TIME RICH

CASH

OPTIONAL

TIME RICH

CASH

OPTIONAL

AN UNCONVENTIONAL GUIDE TO HAPPINESS

CLIFF HARVEY

Katoa Health Publishing

Published by Katoa Health Publishing (CC Publishing), a division of
CC Industries Ltd.

7 Ascension Place, Rosedale, Auckland 0632, NZ

Visit our Web site at www.KatoaHealth.com

ISBN 978-0-473-18288-5

First Edition

Cover design by Amie Tilton

ACKNOWLEDGEMENTS

I wish to thank all those who inspired, nurtured and encouraged me including several of my closest friends and mentors, who are all shining examples of living and loving life: Kent, Chris and Matt Brooks; the Ashendens; and my fight coach and brother Wilf Betz.

My family, who are always an unwavering source of love and support, be they Harveys, Chandlers, Moltzers or Edmondses, and my 'second' families – the Brooks and Walden clans. Mike, Devo and Annie you were a bigger part of this than you realise. Ian, your sage counsel has always had a profound effect on me.

Uncle Dexter – you left us too soon, but the memory of your love for life drives me to be better day-by-day. I stand in the shadow of a great man.

My clients and patients – you fill my days with joy and laughter.

Thanks always to my dad and my sister Charlene – without your tireless support I wouldn't be able to do what I do.

And finally, my fellow spiritual warriors Jason, James, Fraser, Paul, Julien, Mujahid, Marielle, and my Melissas - thanks for walking this path with me.

I love you all.

PROLOGUE

How does one spend years travelling the world?

How does one variously work as a bouncer, a naturopath, nutritionist, strength coach, author, blogger and road manager for a rock and roll band on headlining tours through North America?

How does one find the time to dance, to fight, to wine and dine, to compete in world championships and break world records?

How does one spend one's days healing and helping, being a minister and counsellor to the sick and lost, and one's evenings enjoying fine wine with rock-stars and actors?

Inside these pages I'll show you how I have done all these things and more.

But remember two simple words: *Experiences* and *Time* – because these two words will be the key to a life of freedom you have previously only dreamt of.

This book is about more than actions. It is about actions laid on a foundation of a fundamental change in consciousness – a change in the very paradigm of how we see the world around us and how we relate to the people and things within it.

ABOUT THIS BOOK

GOING BEYOND ACTIONS TO A CONSCIOUS PARADIGM SHIFT

Our current paradigm is not working.

We have fooled ourselves into thinking that accumulating more and more possessions will somehow, at some stage, provide happiness in our lives.

I think most of us realise that this is futile, and yet we keep repeating the same mistakes over and over again. They say that making a mistake is one thing, but repeating it is madness … so perhaps we have all gone a little mad.

It certainly seems that way when we look at how we are depleting the Earth's resources at an ever-increasing rate, polluting our beautiful planet, enslaving other living beings and treating them with appalling cruelty, and becoming, as a species, sicker and more tired.

There's got to be a better way!

And there is.

But to create the change necessary requires more than simply changing actions within the same paradigm we have created. It requires a 'conscious shift' out of the current norm of consumerism and materialism to a mindset of greater simplicity, a mindset where giving is more important than receiving, and a mindset where we have allowed ourselves to dream the lives we want to be living and have rationally evaluated what is *really* necessary to bring that life to fruition.

The economic crisis of the last few years has brought this to the fore for many, and I have seen in clinical health practice and in my lectures and workshops that the people I speak to have really begun re-evaluating what is most important in life. This may well have been the silver lining to the cloud of our most recent economic depression.

We need to re-evaluate life and how we live on a greater scale, and perhaps now we are at a time where a real conscious shift is happening, as more and more people rebel against the norm of working long and hard for little real reward and instead focus on increased happiness and satisfaction.

Our motivation is the primary driver of what we do and is unfortunately provided by the conditioning of the prevailing world paradigm, which is clearly shaped by consumerism and materialism. In fact, I would go so far as to say that the prevailing mentality in the modern world is greed.

And whilst actions of conservation, charity and connection are absolutely crucial to even begin to enact change in the world, there must also be a fundamental shift in consciousness to change the paradigm of *how* we live. We need to begin to recognise what is most important in life – not just that there are problems in the world – and begin to live our lives according to what is most important.

We must absolutely begin to live our lives in a way that does not conform to the processes destroying the planet and reducing the potential of happiness in the world. Our very survival depends upon it.

We need to realise (in the epiphanic sense) that happiness and joy come from joyous experiences – joyous experiences provided by the acts of connection to others, connecting to the world around us, and ultimately connection to that which is greater than us. This aspect of that which is greater than us may be called, in esoteric circles, the super-conscious or divine, but it is being proven more and more regularly, within the realms of emerging sciences such as Noetics, to be an integral and tangible aspect of the physical universe.

Perhaps when there are enough amongst us who are more concerned with people than Prada, a 'tipping point' will occur and the prevailing paradigm will change.

A paradigm of thought is only so because a majority of people believe it, therefore profound, paradigm-shifting change in a very real sense *can* occur when enough people believe in its possibility and begin to act in concert outside the norm. This fundamental change in perception away from status, ego and greed *must* occur in order for us as a species and for the planet as a whole to survive.

The modern sciences are proving again and again that we are all connected, and we are, in turn, connected to everything else on the planet and in the universe. By honouring this we are, by extension, honouring ourselves; conversely by honouring our own health (not just physical but emotional, mental and spiritual) we honour and improve the health of the whole.

I have been asked countless times about my seemingly simplistic attitude that happiness is the goal of an objectively desirable life.

As a health practitioner I have seen that health is equal to happiness! Health of the body is happiness of the body; health of the mind is happiness of the mind and health of the spirit is happiness of the spirit.

And so, although this seems simple, I wonder:

Why not?

Why can't we all be happier?

What is stopping anyone from being healthier and happier?

We all live out our own karma. Certain things *must* occur because events of the past have precipitated them, and often they provide for the learning opportunities we *need* to experience in this lifetime; and yet we can still feel victimised when calamity befalls us. But we have the choice in any given moment to act in ways that improve our circumstances, and we also have a choice to begin to engender more and more the conscious shift that can literally change the entire world and the universe in which it sits.

There is beauty in simplicity. I invite you to be part
of the beautiful change.

HOW TO USE THIS BOOK

Time Rich Cash Optional can simply be read as a book to inspire and motivate, but it also has exercises at the end of every chapter to reinforce the messages and provide opportunities for reflection, and activities to promote real and lasting change. I encourage you to spend some time using the reflections, meditations and activities so that you too can fill your life with a richness of time: the currency of happiness!

Reflections

Spend at least 10 minutes contemplating the reflections at the end of each chapter. Remember that the reflections are tools that help us connect to what is most important in our lives. Sometimes some negative 'stuff' may come up (past hurts, trauma, attachments to self-limiting beliefs etc.), but that is OK. Don't beat yourself up, and don't fall into a victim mentality. Growth and change aren't always easy, and there are learnings and 'growing pains' that are part of the process of self-evolution.

Keep a journal

I suggest keeping a journal specifically for your reflections and exercises from *Time Rich Cash Optional.* In this journal you can keep a note of all your activities and exercises, thoughts and feelings, in the process. It can become a valuable tool for tapping into your creative potential and staying on track.

Contents

INTRODUCTION

I had returned from an extended holiday to South America only to decide to head overseas again – this time to work, live and experience the sights and sounds in Vancouver, Canada.

I told one of my clients – someone I consider a dear friend – of my plans for another trip, to which he replied, "Going away again?! Wow – you must be rich!"

This could not have been any funnier. This guy is extremely successful, very wealthy and, if he chose to, he could travel the world at any time and with few budget restrictions. For him to say that *I* must be rich brought a smile to my lips, and I could not help but have a chuckle.

The reality is that I am not 'rich' in the usual sense of the word. Sure, I have had a modicum of success in various business ventures, and I've had the means to experience the finer things in life – and have also been dead broke! – but what I consider myself to be truly rich in is the most important currency of all: TIME.

I *choose* to travel. I *choose* to take time off 'work' and, in this instance, I was making a powerful choice to travel to a different city to work, live and 'breathe in' a different atmosphere, to meet new and exciting people – and have another adventure. I chose to do this not because I could afford to do it without work, or sacrifice or effort, but instead because I could enrich my life by spending my time on new and exciting experiences.

In the ensuing days several clients, friends and colleagues said things like: "You're so lucky! I wish *I* could travel the world."

(Here's an inside tip for you: *Luck has nothing to do with it.*)

Setting goals, doing the things you want to do and living the life that you want to live are choices.

Choice, not luck, is the key to living the life of your dreams.

Many of my clients are wealthy and successful and could choose to travel the world at any time. That several of them 'wished' that they could, merely shows a lack of inclination to actually *do* something to make those wishes and dreams become a reality. We all make compromises in life, and we all prioritise certain choices. If people are not prepared to do those things they see as wondrous and remarkable, they have chosen that particular path.

And in fact, *any* of my clients (not just the incredibly wealthy ones) could make the choice to travel the world if that is something, they deem to be important to their own life of rich experiences.

But we get tied down in the day-to-day 'money-go-round', and we prioritise things like consumer spending at the expense of experiences.

The fact is that anyone can choose to experience the things they want to experience, and often this costs a lot less than they think.

Open your eyes, look within. Are you satisfied with the life you're living?

~ Bob Marley

The new currency is time, and we all have exactly the same amount to spend – 24 hours of any given day.

How you choose to spend this wealth is up to you.

Time

The only currency that really matters

"TIME IS THE COIN OF YOUR LIFE. IT IS THE
ONLY COIN YOU HAVE, AND ONLY YOU CAN
DETERMINE HOW IT WILL BE SPENT."
~ CARL SANDBURG

What would you say if I asked if you wanted a million dollars?

My guess would be that no matter how wealthy you are, you certainly wouldn't be turning it down.

How about five million dollars?

That's even easier, right?

What if I was to give you a position in one of my companies for the next ten years and offered to pay you ten million dollars at the conclusion of your contract?

But there's a catch …

You have to work for me 16 hours per day, seven days per week.

What was a simple decision (whether or not to accept a vast sum of money) became infinitely more difficult when the variable of *time* was thrown into the equation?

Ten million dollars over ten years at 16 hours per day and seven days per week works out to $171.23 per working hour. Now that's certainly a good wage by most people's standards, but I'm guessing most of you, (and I really hope all of you) like me, wouldn't even consider giving up that much of their time for *any* amount of money.

RETURN ON TIME INVESTMENT

It is common for people to work extremely long hours, doing mentally or physically taxing work in exchange for a considerable income. A particularly good example of this is in the legal field. I once sat down with a friend and tallied up the actual amount of hours he was putting in, both at the office and at home, working for a large, prestigious law firm. When his income was divided by the time he was spending at work, he was actually earning quite a small rate per hour and was by his own admission sacrificing a lot of what he actually wanted to be doing – namely spending time with his wife and young family.

Time is critically important, and it's probably the one thing that people across the board want more of and yet we squander it. Time is the medium in which we can entertain our desires, and having time allows us experiences, joy and love.

Time is the very canvas upon which we paint the story of our lives.

Time allows us to do the things we want to do in order to be the person we want to be.

Life is fleeting and none of us can be certain that we will be here tomorrow. This is not a morbid thought – it's simply the plain, cold truth. And it allows a massive amount of freedom too. If we may not be here tomorrow, we certainly don't want to waste today! And therefore, time is the most important currency we have. Money, on the other hand, is the conduit that allows us to do certain things with our time.

This concept requires that we make a profound shift in our perception of how we value material possessions versus experiences; and it provides a paradigm shift in the entire way we look at life. Time-as-currency actually provides for a very pure form of socialism – one that even the staunchest republican or archconservative could agree with.

I, for one, don't consider myself to belong to any political school or ideology. I am an entrepreneur, and in many ways, I could be described as a pragmatic capitalist – but with a considerable social conscience.

What I mean by this paradigm providing for a form of 'socialism' is that, without the need to institute any systems of governance or restraint, we already have a basic 'set point' of equality in that *we are all born with the same amount of time.*

Each and every one of us has 24 hours in our 'time account' each and every day, and what we choose to do with that time is up to us. How (and whether) we choose to enjoy that time to its fullest is our own choice, and it ultimately determines the quality of the life we will lead.

The Richness of Time

An ample amount of paper wedged between a cover does not make a great book.

In the same way simply having more time does not make a life worth living. The time that we have is the pages upon which we write the legend of our lives (and yes, our lives can and should be worthy of legend).

Simply having more time is not going to give us the joyous experiences that we dream and imagine are part of the life we want to be living. So, it is not enough to have time in abundance (to be 'time rich') but in order to be happier and more in touch with our own personal legend, we must also have a *richness of time.*

Our Dysfunctional Relationship with Time

I was fortunate enough (and honoured) to be invited in 2009 to the Métis National Youth Conference in Vancouver. One of the speakers, elder Tom Brown, stated in one of his workshops that the cause of *all* modern ailments is the clock.

The clock in some form is one of man's oldest inventions. With rudimentary sundials we sought to measure our days, and with hourglasses and water clocks we quantified the passing of time. Not until the modern era though, with the invention of the mechanical clock, were we truly able to divide our days into segments allocated to work, sleep and – sadly it seems – less and less for play.

Where previously time was quantified primarily by the passing of the seasons, the length of the day, state of the moon and by the position of the sun in the sky, the clock allowed time to be quantified on a smaller scale and in a more exact way. This made us more time accountable and therefore provided for a greater amount of time demands upon us.

But what if you had no time constraints when accomplishing a task?

There would be no stress, and as Elder Brown rightly alluded to, *stress is one of the key components contributing to our deteriorating health in the modern world.*

If for example, in the days before clocks, you had to pull your canoe over a mountain, you would simply do it as you were able, without the stress of knowing that you are supposed to have it done by a certain time.

Time accountability is something I mention in this book and in my other writings; however, self-imposed accountability to time is a tool to be used and is a way to free up more time by becoming more effective. We utilise tools, we should not let them negatively affect us. This means that we use the clock to make ourselves time accountable in order to increase our effectiveness. We are then able to do more of what we love and enjoy our breaking moments more.

The nature of time does not change and hasn't ever changed. The only thing that has is the way we have measured and quantified it, and therefore the way we have related to it. And stress is provided, not by scenarios and situations outside of us, but by how we relate to them.

Clocks slay time ... time is dead as long as it is being clicked off by little wheels; only when the clock stops does time come to life.
~ William Faulkner

The Division of Labour

We have been fooled into believing that having a 'good job' and working hard for most of the day, over most days of our lives, is somehow the natural order of things, when in fact the highly specialised division of labour and what we consider to be a 'normal' job are relatively recent inventions.

The Industrial Revolution of the late 1800s drastically altered the type of work performed and the way in which products (and eventually services) were created. Increased specialisation and the greater preponderance of mechanised and process-driven manufacturing plants began to define people, to a greater extent than ever before, as units of work and units of production within a greater whole. In this way workers were seen, and often continue to be seen, as cogs in a machine. Whilst this type of specialisation was essential for allowing the increased productivity necessary for supplying a greater standard of living (at least in a consumer sense) and supplying goods to a rapidly increasing population base, it also had the effect of dehumanising workers.

One could make a valid claim that workers, labourers and farmers before the Industrial Revolution were every bit as downtrodden as their post-Industrial Revolution compatriots (especially in the context of Middle Ages serfdom and later forms of indentured labour) and the conditions that were perhaps accelerated by the Industrial Revolution certainly helped to encourage the growth of communism, unionism and socialist philosophies to protect worker rights.

Regardless, there was a philosophical counterpoint engrained in capitalistic philosophy at the time: that labour is a commodity and people are, in the context of production, merely machines that facilitate labour.

What is worrying now is that we have developed an ideological 'set point' in our modern society that values the stability and security of having a 'job' and that sees value in the idea of the 'Protestant work ethic'. In reality there is little security in jobs and careers in the modern workplace by virtue of the position itself. Technology has taken the place of many of the former functions of various professions and will continue to do so at an increasing rate and affordable, and in many cases highly skilled, immigrant and offshore workers have affected the job security of various trades in many developed nations.

By setting ourselves up as 'parts of the machine' we have opened the door, inevitably, to competition from machines and to the burden of unending cost/price competition. We have fooled ourselves into taking the cues from those in positions of wealth and authority and have in many cases become, to our detriment, merely cogs in the machine of the modern economy.

The Meaning of Money

Money is simply a medium of exchange by which we initially satisfy our needs and then our wants.

In the earliest days of hominoid existence every person or family/tribal unit satisfied all of their survival needs by scavenging, hunting and gathering what was required.

The earliest forms of trade provided for a new level of expediency. There may not always have been an abundance of certain resources in an area, so by trading with others, tribes of early humans could satisfy more of their needs and wants through a bartering economy. This not only helped individual groups but was also an example of the continued evolution of the species. Trading allowed a greater degree of connection with others from outside the immediate familial and tribal unit. Over time this allowed greater and greater levels of specialisation which further encouraged greater interdependence and therefore connection between groups and individuals.

With these increasingly deeper levels of specialisation there came a need to provide a medium of exchange, so commodity-based, and later representative currency became the accepted norm and evolved into the system we now have, in which money is simply a shared value set that we all adhere to.

Chapter 1 Exercises:

Calculate your ROTI

People are often surprised when they evaluate just how much time they are putting into their work and how little they are actually earning when compared to that time.

This exercise is not designed to cast a negative light on what you do. I know for myself that I willingly put a *lot* of time into what I do, sometimes for little reward – but I love doing it. The value of this exercise comes from having a concrete idea of your 'return on time investment' so you can then ask yourself some important questions.

- Tally up *all* the time you spend in the pursuit of your job. Include travelling time, time that you spend attending work functions outside of work hours that you wouldn't attend for enjoyment's sake, and any overtime or additional work time you devote to your job.
- Divide your gross annual income by the amount of time (in hours) you spend working.
- This is your ROTI figure.

Do you feel this amount is enough to justify the time and effort expended? Does your love for what you do decrease or increase *your* perception of your monetary ROTI?

What is your relationship with money?

Our relationship with money can inadvertently derail our attempts to enjoy our time.

- Get a *big* sheet of paper and some pens (or crayons, pencils – whatever you feel most comfortable and most creative writing with!).
- Spend a few minutes relaxing – breath steadily and gently allow yourself to become calm.
- Write the words 'MONEY IS' in the middle of your sheet and then around it write any words or draw any images or concepts that come to mind.
- Spend at least 10 minutes putting down on your sheet all thoughts that come into your mind .
- When 10 minutes are up look at your sheet. What does it say about your relationship with money?

Do you see money as a tool that you can use to achieve your dream life?

Are there negative feelings and emotions attached to your relationship with money?

Do you see money as a goal rather than a means to *help* attain the things that *really* matter?

Reflections

Do you feel you never have enough time? Why?

Are you enjoying your time and your work, or are you waiting for the time when you will be 'able' to enjoy your life?

Are you indispensable to your work, or could you be replaced by a machine or low-cost employee?

(And don't worry – we will work on any negatives coming out of these exercises and reflections over the rest of the book!)

CHAPTER TWO

Joyous Experience

The philosophy of the time rich

"FILL YOUR LIFE WITH AS MANY MOMENTS AND EXPERIENCES OF JOY AND PASSION AS YOU HUMANLY CAN. START WITH ONE EXPERIENCE AND BUILD ON IT."
~ MARCIA WIEDER

What is the point of life?

We have all, like the great philosophers throughout time, pondered this question.

When you cut back any philosophy or religion to its most basic and fundamental level, it is the search for answers and explanations of the happenings of the world around us, and on a deeper and more profound level, an attempt to answer the greater question: What is it all about?

Philosophical schools, although appearing divergent, tend to have more common ground than disparity. I have always had the idea that what we *do* is so much more important than anything else, so I always had a saying: 'Talk is cheap, and dreams are free. We are defined by our actions.' And although I think this is fundamentally true, I have begun to add a caveat to it: 'Talk is cheap, and dreams are free. We are defined by our actions, but sometimes need to be judged by our intentions.' This caveat helps to 'round out', to make a little more pragmatic, this broad philosophical statement.

Take this example: I walk into the kitchen and open the fridge door to grab a snack. After pulling out some yoghurt and berries I slam the fridge door, just as you happen to put your head down to also look in the fridge. In the process I give you a nasty knock to the head.

Now in this instance the action undoubtedly had a negative result (you got whacked in the head!). But if I am to be judged for this, we need to look at my intention as well as the result of my action. There are some very different scenarios here. I may have been simply unaware that you were about to bend down and look in the fridge and I accidentally shut the door, inadvertently causing you pain. No big deal, I'm sorry, you forgive me and after a hug we're back to being friends. A polar situation, though, could be that I saw you bending down to look in the fridge and, seizing my opportunity, slammed the door into your head – which of course is not cool!

You can see that my intention, when known, changes how my actions are perceived, and in turn how *I* am perceived as a result of my actions. If I had wanted to hurt you, it would have been malicious on my part – not very virtuous at all – so the perceptions held by others plainly can, and perhaps should, be affected by their judging of our intention. Action though is something that is plainly evident, and if you are living as you'd like to live, you will also be defined by that in the perception of others. To be honest, even if you are not it is a moot point because you are doing what you *must* in order to live your own personal life of fulfilment.

And yet the question remains: *What is the point of life?*

I have been called naive and simplistic when I state, quite plainly (and yes – simply) that the point of life is to be *happy*.

We all – each and every one of us – strive to be happy. We seek out experiences, people and *things* that we think will make us happier. Of course, we often choose the wrong things, the wrong people and the wrong experiences – those that don't lead to any lasting or escalating happiness – but nonetheless we try and try again to bring greater amounts of joy into our lives. Conversely, we quite justifiably seek to minimise harm to ourselves and to avoid situations that are going to reduce our joy and happiness.

This brings us to an interesting junction. If we agree that our lives and our 'selves' are defined by our actions, and if we are to be judged by our intentions, we are presented with a question of ethics: *What defines 'right' action?*

If happiness is at least a large part of the puzzle of what constitutes an objectively desirable life, then it stands to reason that what is most right is that which creates the greatest amount of happiness.

VIRTUE & HAPPINESS

Eudaemonia (happiness) and *arete* (virtue) are the two central concepts of Ancient Greek ethics.

Eudaemonia is often directly translated into English as 'happiness', but this is not entirely accurate as the concept of *eudaemonia* is broader and involves not just happiness but greater concepts of wellness and directly relates to an objectively desirable life.

Eudaemonism is the moral theory that links *arete* with *eudaemonia* (virtue with happiness), so eudaemonism in a nutshell is 'the virtue of happiness'.

We can see that there is, in the concept of eudaemonism, a correlation between virtue and happiness, and this can provide a guide for what we do in our lives.

Socrates, Plato, Epicurus and, perhaps most importantly, Aristotle and the Stoics provided definitions for and theorised various nuances of the form of eudaemonism. In Aristotle's *Nicomachean Ethics*, *eudaemonia* is considered the highest aim of human thinking and endeavour and is something that is achieved through action (of the *psyche* or soul). Aristotelian ethics was considered by Aristotle himself to be unique, in that it was extremely practical rather than simply theoretical.

A NEW EUDAEMONISM

A new paradigm of eudaemonism (or what I have called for expediency 'neoeudaemonism') is a simple one. 'Right action' is that which promotes happiness and therefore what is 'most right' is that which promotes the greatest amount of net happiness.

And so, this neoeudaemonism can be summed up succinctly as either a 'law of ethics' –

That which is most right is that which creates the greatest net happiness.

or as a 'razor' –

The 'rightness' of an action is determined by how much happiness that action creates.

This bears similarities to utilitarianism, although the idea of 'pleasure' seems to be more ubiquitous in utilitarianism whereas 'happiness' is perhaps a fundamentally more complete, global and holistic ideal for ethics, as we shall see.

HAPPINESS V. ECSTASY

The question arises that if 'right action' is concerned with creating happiness, then does that mean we should be selfish and simply do whatever is best for us in any given situation?

The reality we have all experienced is that selfishness and greed *do not* make us happy. They provide for a transient amount of ecstasy, but lasting happiness does not occur and there is no elevation in our total levels of happiness, and certainly no elevation in the happiness of those around us (the victims of our greed). There is, in effect, a *net loss* in happiness when we are selfish, due to several factors:

Guilt

The guilt associated with doing wrong by another person only serves to diminish one's happiness. The long-term effect is an erosion of intrinsic satisfaction, a reduction in feelings of personal virtue and self-worth, and an increasing desire for further escape and distraction through transient states of ecstasy. These states can be found in drugs, alcohol and sexual promiscuity, and through wanton greed and materialism.

Karma

If we treat people poorly it is bound to come back to us at some stage.

People remember being wronged, and at the very least they will not want to deal with you again. People talk, and others may be less inclined to be associated with you, to trust you and to take you into their confidence. Overall this results in a *big* reduction in connection and happiness. We also reflect subtly, via energetic pathways and as a result of subconscious recognition of pheromones and visual (body language and facial) cues, the way that others act. When we act inappropriately to others, it will be reflected back immediately to us.

Escalating needs for pleasure

The more we lie, cheat and steal for personal gain, and the more we seek transient states of ecstasy, the more we need to do these things to provide any degree of fulfilment.

Materialism and greed are very much like drugs. Just as a junkie needs to have more and more of a drug in order to get the same fix, people who are addicted to 'things' need more and more of those things in order to try and seek the satisfaction they are looking for. How many people stay satisfied with the same car for any length of time? Be it a Ferrari, a Porsche or a Toyota there comes a point very shortly after taking possession when it becomes 'just a car'.

MONEY DOES NOT EQUAL HAPPINESS

Most of us know and accept this simple concept. In fact, we all hear people saying various versions of this statement in our day-to-day lives, but most people *live* in a way that indicates that the deeper meaning they *believe* is that money is not necessarily equal to happiness, but they still would be markedly happier if they had more money.

In my experience, most people feel that perhaps they could be happy and poor but would really be much happier rich. However, the reality, backed up time and again by research, is that we need to be able to satisfy our survival and social 'needs' in order to reach a critical level of happiness, but over and above this amount there is no increase in happiness levels at all. In other words, it has been shown that up to a certain point in income level, people are generally less happy, but there is a critical tipping point at which most day-to-day needs can be comfortably met. Happiness levels rise as income approaches this point, but there is no further rise after it. So, the old adage that 'you can be happy and poor or happy and rich' is very apt.

I'm not suggesting that you should be poor, far from it; however, the overall key to living a joyful life is happiness itself, and happiness is the ability to have moment upon moment of joyous experience. We could also say that having more time to devote to joyous experience is crucial to this. Research provides an interesting anomaly on this point too.

A nationwide Bureau of Labour Statistics report in the US[1] showed that people with higher incomes devoted greater amounts of their time to 'obligatory' activities (such as work,

---

[1] http://www.bls.gov/news.release/archives/atus_06242009.htm

shopping and childcare) and that these activities (especially work) equated to greater stress levels. Lower income groups, by comparison, devoted nearly twice as much time to leisure activities and as a consequence had lower stress levels. What this study doesn't show well is the *quality* of time and leisure activities, but it does offer an interesting counterpoint for the argument that wealth by its very nature provides for greater leisure time. In fact, wealth could be seen as inconsequential for increasing leisure time and the demands of work to garner wealth could in fact preclude it.

The Western Misconception of

Happiness & Wealth

Several surveys of happiness indices of nations also point to a misconception amongst the most developed nations that wealth is equated with happiness.

The World Values Survey of 2003, of people in 65 nations, was published in the British magazine *New Scientist*. The survey found that the world's happiest countries with the most satisfied people are Puerto Rico and Mexico, and those with the most optimistic people are Nigeria and Mexico. These relatively poor nations (and others) consistently outperform wealthier countries like the USA (16th on the list) and have significantly lower rates of depression. Diagnostic differences aside, there is still a body of evidence suggesting that perhaps the wealth we in the West consider to be crucial to a happy, healthy lifestyle is in fact based on a fallacy.

Veteran journalist Richard Ernsberger wrote in a July 2004 article in *Newsweek International*:

We Americans are told in our Declaration of Independence that three things are sacrosanct – "life, liberty, and the pursuit of happiness." And like fellow hedonists in Asia, Europe and elsewhere, we've clearly taken the message to heart. We work hard, earn lots of money and spend gleefully on iPods, flat-screen TVs, SUVs and all sorts of expensive fripperies. We indulge, we gratify – and therefore we expect to be the happiest damn people on the planet. So why aren't we?

Indeed, with all the material wealth and consumer items that the majority of us now have and spend our hard-earned money on, *why aren't we happier?*

Have we got it all wrong?

Have we lost sight of what truly makes us happy?

Intrinsic Reward, Extrinsic Reward and Happiness

The perception that wealth will improve our happiness is predicated on a foundation of extrinsic reward. Wealth begets material possessions, and the ability to procure and amass these possessions, one might assume, should make us happier than had we not gained them; however, this isn't the case. Procuring possessions does not increase happiness at all. Possessions are only the 'conduits' or 'tools' we use in the various actions of creating moments of joy. We only feel better when we create an escalating amount of happiness. When we can bring joy into our lives, as well as the lives of others, we begin to create a cascade that changes the world we live in and by extension we begin to affect the total happiness of the entire world.

There is a big difference between what is intrinsically rewarding and what is extrinsically rewarding. Most of the things we find 'intrinsically' rewarding are experiential in nature, and most of what is extrinsically rewarding has its basis in material possessions. We find things internally or intrinsically rewarding in and of themselves, whereas things that require an external reward require the appreciation and recognition of others. We can therefore see that extrinsic reward is based solely on the ultimately futile pursuit of attempting to satisfy the ever-needier ego. When we rely on the thoughts and perceptions of others to try and create our happiness it will never be great or lasting; however, creating a life of meaningful experiences will elevate one's happiness to greater and greater levels. Extrinsic reward can also come in the form of manipulating others for personal gain and in the abuse of drugs, and these only ever lead to a brief flash of ecstasy and a fulfilment that is transitory at best.

The only way to create lasting happiness in our lives is to create connections with others and to live a life of joyous experience.

Use the razor in daily decision-making

For the next few days, if you have a decision to make try using the 'happiness razor' to help guide you to a decision. If presented with several options, consider which would create the greatest amount of total happiness (for *all* parties involved).

Recognising hurt and releasing guilt

One thing that affects our ability to be happy more than perhaps anything else is guilt. It plays on and on in our subconscious and causes anxiety and stress patterns that can continue even when we don't consciously realise, they are there.

- Start by imagining your life at the earliest possible point (this should be conception or close to it).

- Slowly imagine through your life from start to now, all the times when you have done something that hurt somebody else (this can include animals) and that you still feel guilty about.

- Consider how you acted and how it affected the other person.

- Forgive yourself. Actually, say the words to yourself: "I forgive myself for this past imperfection."

- Release any remaining guilt and tension. You can do this by saying: "I release all remaining guilt and tension from this past imperfection" then take a deep breath in, and as you breathe out, let all the inner turmoil, guilt and tension be released with the breath.

- Finish each of these reminiscences by giving thanks to the person or animal that you have wronged and sending your love to them: "I thank you for the lesson you have provided me. I love you."

Reflections

Do the 'toys' and gadgets I have bought in the past give me any real pleasure now?

Do I believe I'd be happier if I were rich? Why do I believe this? Is it justified? Is there anything stopping me from being happy now?

Really? Are you sure?

CHAPTER THREE

Becoming Unconventional

Why being normal doesn't work

"YOU SEE THE OLD WAY WASN'T WORKIN',
SO IT'S ON US TO DO WHAT WE GOTTA
DO…TO SURVIVE."
~ TUPAC SHAKUR

If you are not living the way you would like to, you have to ask yourself: Why not?

Whatever you are doing is leading to a set of results. If those results are not the ones you want, then you obviously have to change your actions.

A huge challenge arises when, even though we are doing all the things we have been told by our parents, educators and people in positions of power in business and society, we are still not living the life we want to be living. Our education system is predicated around providing normal, stable, willing workers for the machinery of society – but being a normal, stable, willing worker is not what this book is about! This book is about living a life of playfulness, passion and purpose.

If the norm is telling you that you should be a certain way, live a certain way and work a certain way, and it's not making you happy, then the norm isn't working for *you*. The only option is to step outside the norm and be prepared to set your own rules and specify your own definitions of success in order to live the life that *you* want to live.

Taking this step is not easy. We have been told over countless years that normal is good and abnormal is bad. We have been conditioned, and we have told ourselves that 'fitting in' is the best way to progress in life. The problem is that *this isn't even remotely true.*

Fitting in is safe. Fitting in provides the anonymity to fly 'below the radar' and not open yourself up to criticism; however, no one who ever changed the world did so by being normal. Normal is simply … well … normal! Revolutionaries in any field are by nature 'outliers'. They are the people prepared not to conform to the status quo, and as a result are able to influence and change the status quo. Without these luminaries and visionaries there would be no society, no culture and none of the progress that makes the human species so amazing and fascinating.

Our Primal Fear:

Stepping Outside the Norm

As human beings we have an amazing potential for survival. Our survival responses are finely tuned and extremely pervasive. We often don't even realise the extent to which our subconscious mind, our primal urges and instincts and our conditioning affect our day-to-day actions. But rest assured, they do, and one of the most important things we have garnered as a species is our ability to improve our survival through collective security. This collective security of living in groups and having strength in numbers also means we don't want to put ourselves in situations where we might be criticised and potentially ostracised.

Of course, nowadays being somewhat ostracised is really no big deal, but in a primal setting if we were ostracised from our tribe, it could be a huge hindrance to our further survival. If we were to say things and act in ways that were considered too radical in a primal setting, we would risk being ejected from our tribal grouping and thereby have to survive alone in the wild. What is 'radical' is deemed by default to be 'dangerous' for the simple reason that if you are surviving by doing something a certain way, that is deemed at a subconscious level to be a safe and appropriate set point of behaviour. Actions and thoughts outside of this set point are unknown, have greater risk and are therefore potentially dangerous and counter to survival.

This is the reason that public speaking and performing are so greatly feared by so many. We still hold on to the pattern of not wanting to 'step outside the norm' in front of our peers because our primal instincts tell us we may put ourselves at risk if we do. So, to forge a unique and fulfilling life we really need to accept that we may need to step outside the norm. The safety of conformity comes to naught if we are unable to achieve our dreams and goals because of it.

We have already realised that the old paradigm of being 'rich' is not working in and of itself (to make us happy) so we need to make a decision to have more time and richness within our time, rather than simply having more money.

Someone whom I would consider truly rich has leveraged their time and income effectively so that they are able to do things they want to do and do the things that bring joyous experience to themselves, the people around them and the world at large. Often those we traditionally consider 'wealthy' actually have less time than those considered 'poor'. I have known many people who I would consider truly rich, and they are not necessarily the people others would consider rich but they all live lives of wonder and joy. They have time in abundance, and they fill that time with experiences that make themselves *and others* happy. Some work pretty hard and some work very hard and long, others don't *work* (in the traditional sense) at all, but all of them spend their allotment of time –

their 24 hour, daily 'time pay-check' – according to *their rules* alone. These people range from energy healers to property tycoons to part-time, semi-professional athletes and rock musicians.

Moreover, the old idea of being 'rich' just simply doesn't make sense anymore (if it ever really did) because it is: a) not sustainable for the planet, and b) doesn't necessarily bring us what we need (joyous experience and happiness). For what good are riches without experiences and what joy is there in a life lived for work?

Many people are now living according to a new paradigm of wealth and success, and there are very real differences in the life afforded through this new paradigm. If we examine the old and new paradigms of what is considered 'rich' or 'successful' we can see some striking differences:

Old Paradigm	New Paradigm
Have a lot of money	Have time and energy to spend on experiences
Work as a means to an end	Enjoy their work and use to provide the means to do the things they want to do
Have a 'deferred life plan'	Are not prepared to wait to live the life they want to live
Possessions provide status and escape	Possessions are tools that allow experiences
Leverage their money to make more money	Leverage money to create more time for experiences and allow more varied and rich experiences

TRAPS AND PITFALLS OF THE 'OLD PARADIGM'

Trap #1: Working to make 'money'

But Cliff, we all work to make money! What are you talking about?

While it's true that we all work to make money, the intention behind this is what's important.

Ask yourself: *Is money important in and of itself?*

Of course, it's not! Money is just paper, disks of metal or a string of numbers on a statement or in the ether. There is no tangible importance attached to money as an 'object' at all. In a very literal sense, there has been no physical 'value' to money since the dissolution of the last vestiges of the gold standard resulting from the 'Nixon Shock' of the early seventies[2]. In a completely objective sense, even gold has no real inherent value (especially as its perceived value is predicated on the demand created by its use in jewellery and ornamentation, a value which in a survival situation would very quickly evaporate).

There is only importance attached to the 'concept' of money. We share a collective belief in the value of money, and we influence this value through the machinations of local and global economics. In effect, money is a metaphor for the things it can buy. Its value is underpinned by the idea of things we

---

[2] http://en.wikipedia.org/wiki/Gold_standard#Post-war_international_gold-dollar_standard_.281946.E2.80.931971.29

believe we would enjoy, and therefore it is a conduit for experience only – plain and simple, nothing more and nothing less.

So, *do you really work to 'make money'?*

Or is it the things you can do with that money that are truly important?

I'm not denying that some amongst us have financial goals defined by a dollar amount of cash, savings or investments but this at best is still a 'way point', along the path towards the life they want to live.

This reminds me of a conversation with my friend and mentor, business author Dr Ian Brooks, who told me of a speaking appearance he had in the USA. Attending this conference were several 'big shots' from the oil industry. When he asked them what business they were in they immediately said, "Oil!"

Of course, they *are* in the business of selling oil. But Ian prompted them further. "But what are you REALLY selling?" to which they incredulously replied something along the lines of, "Boy … we already told ya … we sell OIL!"

The problem here, and what Ian was getting at, is that to the customers the oil itself is relatively inconsequential. Oil is horrible, black, smelly stuff. No one in their right mind wants to buy oil for oil's sake. But oil provides the means by which people can take out their boats, get to work and take their families away for holidays. Like money, it is a conduit for experience. And money is the most basic of all conduits, as it provides the means by which we purchase the other conduits of experience (like oil) that enrich our lives.

Unless you are Scrooge McDuck, money itself has no intrinsic value. Sure, you could paper your walls with it, or you could make some pretty funky artistic collages with it. But the value of money is in what we can do with it.

We don't work for 'money'. We work so that the money we make can work for us and provide us with experiences.

Trap #2: Having a deferred life plan

Most people long for the day that they can sit back and relax and either do a whole lot of nothing or do some of the things they have always wanted to do. In order to accomplish this, they work hard for a long period of time until they reach that golden time known as 'retirement'. This is the traditional way that many in society work and is what I and many others call a 'deferred life plan'.

Some people have wonderful, fulfilling retirements, but usually these *aren't* the same people who completely deferred their goals and dreams, so they actually managed to *live* and not put all their hopes, dreams and aspirations on hold. Put simply, they didn't live their lives according to a deferred life plan.

Many people, however, find themselves at the end of their working lives sick and tired and unable to do many of the things they had dreamt of doing. They also find themselves so patterned and defined by their lives of working for so long that they are lost when they finally have free time. The time that was supposed to be set aside to do all those things they wanted to do is instead wasted, as they either have lost sight of what it was that they wanted to do, or have become physically, mentally or emotionally unable to do those things. Ironically, in these cases, time has been wasted in a paradoxical pursuit of time, and quality of time has been destroyed – both in the moments of wasted time throughout life, and by the activities and choices of the person's life that degraded their health and physical condition.

We also defer in smaller ways, on a day-to-day and week-to-week basis. How many people do you know who *live for the weekends*? I bet you wouldn't have enough fingers to count them. *Living for the weekend* is a common trap, but it is one born of not doing something that you love, and not finding joy in the moments of your day-to-day routine, but instead trying to find it in the bottom of a bottle in a bar or club at three in the morning on Friday or Saturday night.

People who value their time and who aren't prepared to live a life of mediocrity do not subscribe to the deferred life plan. Instead they *plan* for the future but *live* in the moment. They plan to do the things they have always wanted to do as soon as they are able, not when an arbitrary paradigm dictates that they should.

Take something as simple as travelling. This is one of the most highly prized conduits of experience, but also one of the main things that people put off until retirement. Even when we plan to travel sooner, there are so many times when we find ourselves searching for the 'right' time to travel and continue putting it off as new projects, tasks and responsibilities come up.

Here's the reality though: *those things never cease arising.* For as long as you are there to receive them, people will always provide commitments for you to fill. Your job will always provide new tasks, and there will always be events and goings-on to fill your precious time.

In order to do anything at all you simply have to set goals, set a time frame and do it!

There is only ever one moment that we live in, and that is the present, so if there are things we want to do, and have the ability to do, shouldn't we be doing them? *For if not now …when?*

Trap #3: Working for work's sake

Along with living to a deferred life plan comes the trap of working for work's sake.

Without goals, dreams and aspirations, what are we working for? What are we working towards?

The answer is: *Who knows?*

If you haven't analysed the things you want to do and have, you won't know how much to work and what to do for work in order to achieve them. Instead of working doing something you love, or at the very least finding joy in aspects of your work, and working towards having experiences, you instead end up working in order to enjoy the weekends and buy gadgets, trinkets and toys to try and catch some fleeting degree of happiness. And whilst these things can give some level of transient distraction, there never really is any lasting enjoyment, and at the end of the day you are left with an expensive piece of plastic, metal or cloth that compels you to do *something* with it.

Trap #4: Possessions that possess us

Unless we have an idea about who we want to be, what we want to do and achieve, and the type of life we want to be living, it is absolutely impossible to know what possessions, what 'things' we need to acquire to make that a reality.

Most people acquire possessions for three reasons:

1.   Status

Much of how we are perceived in the world is unfortunately dictated by what we 'have'.

We can of course choose to either play this game or not. If the context of one's life is not defined by what they want to be doing and by the person they want to be, but is instead dictated by the expectations of others, they can fall easily into the trap of acquiring things for the purely extrinsic (but fleeting) rewards of social status and perception.

2.   Diversion

The other reason people amass 'things' is to divert themselves. Several factors precipitate this. The most important is that if we don't know what we are trying to achieve in life, we have no idea what we need to have in order to get there. And if we don't know what we need to have it is tempting to try and divert ourselves with toys. PlayStation, Wii, jet skis and myriads of other toys can provide us with transient distraction. And hey, if you love playing Wii then that is the absolute best reason to get one – several years ago I became quite enamoured with *Rock Band®*! – but if you don't know what you love doing, if the Wii is simply a means of distraction because you are bored or depressed, there may be better things to do with your time, and better things to spend your money on – for you.

An extremely wealthy and successful client of mine had all the toys in the world. A brand new $180,000 SUV, jet skis, land yachts, boats, quad bikes … you name it, he had it. He was a very 'experiential' guy and looking in from the outside he appeared to genuinely enjoy all the toys he had. But over the years that I worked with him; a strange thing *happened. He began to get rid of all his toys, one by one. After he sold the jet skis went the quad bikes, then the land yachts, the boat — and the SUV spent more time in the garage than it did on the road.*

One day while we were hanging out, he said, "You know, Cliff, all those things were just too much stress. I always felt compelled to have to use them … it was almost as if my possessions had begun to possess me!"

Each and every one of his toys was not a negative thing in its own right, but the intention behind buying them was inherently flawed from day one. They had all been bought as a means of distraction. The difference comes down to knowing the life you want to live. This allows you to acquire the things you need to make that life a reality, and to have the possessions that are the tools of joyous experience as compared to simply seeing a new gadget and then creating a fantasy of what it could bring into your life.

Boredom is one of the biggest reasons for needing distraction. Let's face it, if we are engaged doing things we love doing, filling our time with something else doesn't even cross our minds. Because I *love* to do many things (like writing, speaking, ju-jitsu, weightlifting, wandering, wondering, reading, poetry, art … and the list goes on) I have plenty of things that bring me joy. When I want to do nothing, I can do that too. Distraction from boredom doesn't really rear its ugly head, unless of course I have fallen into a period of being goal-less and of being aim-less.

When we know the life that we want to be living, and we are in fact living it, we have a context for how to spend our time and know what we need to acquire, so we don't fall into the trap of acquiring possessions for distraction or status.

3.   Social and cultural conditioning

This is to me the most interesting reason that we amass possessions. We live in a society that has been shaped over thousands upon thousands of years. Over time, any culture, system and society develops norms of behaviour that most people, most of the time, accept without question. These norms often end up dictating at least a portion of the things we feel we must 'have'.

Two lifestyle examples from my time in Vancouver, British Columbia highlighted this to me.

I had been living in Vancouver for about a winter and we were moving into summer. I was leaving my apartment for my daily stroll to the beach to meditate, write, soak up the sun and share some moments with interesting (and hopefully female) Vancouverites. Just as I was stepping out the door my roommate said, somewhat incredulously, "What? No shoes!" At that moment it dawned on me that people in my new city just didn't walk around barefoot. Not that they do on the whole in my home country of Aotearoa (New Zealand) but it certainly seems to be more common – particularly in summer.

As I strolled barefoot to the beach, I became aware that I had begun to go out barefoot less because it wasn't the norm in my new hometown. Without realising it I had begun to conform to a cultural and societal norm that was at odds with my own ideas of health and wellness. This realisation made me more mindful of my own activities, and I began to walk, jog and train barefoot as I had most of my life, even in the middle of the Canadian winter.

Being outside of the norm certainly gave me some local notoriety, and I continue to get a few strange looks from passers-by. I was even stopped by the police on one occasion for walking barefoot! But I believe that walking barefoot is better for me, physiologically, and is an important part of my personal spiritual practice, so for me to be outside the norm is the right choice for me.

But what does barefoot walking and running have to do with money, possessions and being 'Time Rich'?

Actually, a lot; you see, by walking and jogging barefoot I don't need to acquire the possessions that many people need to have to enjoy these activities – namely shoes.

I do have shoes – in fact I really like sneakers – and I have at times had quite a collection, particularly as I was sponsored for a long time by athletic apparel companies. But I don't wear them often, so I don't need to replace them often either. I certainly don't need running shoes or hiking boots, as I never wear them anyway, and by not conforming to that particular societal norm – one that is at odds with my own ideology – I am able to eliminate an unnecessary cost burden.

This concept was made even more apparent by another example from my own life which I will relate via a post from my blog (www.cliffdog.com):

I was sitting in my room the other day thinking 'Something isn't right here …'

I had been having a feeling for some time that I needed to reorganise my living space to create more space and more flow. From time to time I seek to improve the Feng Shui of my bedroom, and whilst I'm no expert on that topic, I've certainly found it helps my mental space to have a decluttered physical space. So, I shifted my bed — the largest piece of furniture in my room — and set about trying to arrange other items in a way that was more conducive to both physical and energetic flow when it suddenly hit me …

I don't need a bed!

I realised that I had this big ol' bed in the middle of my room and if I got rid of it there would be a heck of a lot more space — and a lot more flow.

The bed I had cost me an arm and a leg, but it is also WAY too soft for me (long story — bought for the benefit of a former bed mate more than for me). I have always preferred harder mattresses and so figured there could be a valuable experiment in sleeping on the floor, as there's not much harder than that. I also do believe that our bodies acclimate to sleeping on harder surfaces over time, and given enough time to adapt, long term it may be more beneficial for our posture. My neck, which has sustained some weightlifting and wrestling injuries, has certainly suffered as a result of sleeping on a soft mattress for the last few years.

And so, in typically Cliff fashion, I took the bed into the basement without further ado, prepared to give this next experiment in unconventional living a fair shot.

Over the next few nights I noticed that I slept better. It was cooler on the floor (I usually get really hot at night) and my neck felt far less strain. The only negative was that my hip dug into the floor when I rolled over – but this was dealt with by putting a couple of extra blankets on the floor. I also noticed that I slept for a shorter period of time but had better quality of sleep. The shortened sleep I can only think is because of the increased quality, less heat and less neck and back strain.

I now have a thin bed roll made up of some thick blankets and sheets on the floor which I roll out at night and roll away in the morning. It gives me: a) a better night's sleep, b) more space to work, meditate and do yoga in my room, and c) a less cluttered feel to my room – plus perhaps if I find myself couch surfing, sleeping rough or otherwise bed-less, I'll already be acclimatised to it!

It's been several weeks now and thus far I can only see positives from being barefoot and bed-less;– however, as some of my friends and colleagues have pointed out, potential bed mates may prefer to sleep in a bed – and the antics of 'floor action' only seem appealing to the fairer sex when it is an option, not an ultimatum.

Oh well – such are the choices for vagabonds and raconteurs who choose to live a life of adventuring in the unconventional!

The interesting point here is that I will never again *need* a bed. What is considered a must-have for most people is not even an issue for me. Whether to have a bed at all is completely inconsequential, and there is no effect on my quality of life at all. In fact, due to my sleeping better and having more space, my quality of life is improved. I also have eliminated one of the major annoyances of moving a bed when changing locations and the financial burden of buying a bed.

By moving outside the norm where it suits our highest good and fits with our own ideology and philosophy of life, we reduce our dependence on material possessions.

Trap #5: Leveraging money to make more money

Like working for the sake of working, or working for money's sake, the old rich paradigm involves leveraging money (in the form of investments) to make more money. This is only a valid paradigm where the increase in wealth is necessary for increased life satisfaction. Money is a conduit for security, and it's a conduit for experiences, so we do need to create enough financial solidity if we are to have these. If we can leverage our money in order to more effectively allow more *time* for us, then it is in line with our 'Time Rich' goals. However, if it is leveraging for the sake of simply having more and more money in our bank accounts, then we have fallen back into the old Scrooge-like hoarding mentality, which is a waste of our effort and a waste of our precious time.

I have been associated with many extremely wealthy people over the years, many of whom were extremely pragmatic, some of whom were wonderfully philanthropic ... and a few who simply couldn't see the wood for the trees.

I remember being at a cocktail party. I was a young, up-and-coming businessman in the health and wellness field. I was happy to be amongst a group of people who, to my young mind, had 'made it'. I was drifting between conversations, talking with the people I knew – colleagues and clients – and meeting others I didn't know. I stumbled on a conversation between several of this region's wealthiest people. And you would never guess what they were talking about ... *how much money they had in the bank*. I kid you not!

They weren't even talking about it in obtuse or cryptic ways. They were each going on, and on ... and on ... about how much cold, hard cash they had sitting in their bank accounts. You just can't make this stuff up. There was one thought that went through my mind: *Wow, you guys are ... BORING!*

With all the money they had, surely they could have been discussing any number of topics: how they were trying to help others with their inordinate wealth; all the fun things they were doing to enjoy their lives; how they were enriching the lives of their families and friends because they have the means to do so ... but no, the only thing they deemed worthy of discussion was how much money they had. I quite quickly left the conversation and thanked my lucky stars that I hadn't, and never would, let the trap of the love of wealth for wealth's sake make me a boring 'non-vagabond'.

*"**Normal** is getting dressed in clothes that you buy for work and driving through traffic in a car that you are still paying for - in order to get to the job you need to pay for the clothes and the car, and the house you leave vacant all day so you can afford to live in it."*

~ Ellen DeGeneres

REMOVE 'SHOULD' FROM YOUR VOCABULARY

The word *should* is one of the least powerful words we have in the English language, but one that is extremely commonly used – in fact it's the 205th most commonly used word in English[3].

Should is a future-centred word that denotes separation and extrinsic motivation and encourages guilt.

I often ask clients, "Do you meditate?" I ask this to get some context for their spiritual practice, relaxation etc. – not in any way to make them feel guilty, for it doesn't matter to me whether they meditate or not. It's a choice for them to make based on the life they want to be leading.

There are no absolutes in life; however, in the vast majority of cases, if they aren't meditating, they seem embarrassed and say something along the lines of: "I really *should ..."*

Why should you?

Who says you should?

---

[3] http://www.world-english.org/english500.htm

Should ALWAYS replaces the positive aspects of what we *want and need* to be doing for our highest interest with a negative extrinsic compulsion that is both limiting and self-defeating.

There are no rules, and if you are living an unconventional life there is no one to tell you what to do, nor anyone to compel you to do things based on what is considered to be the right course of action. If you want to do something, then do it. If you don't, then don't. And if you feel that you should do something because it will take you closer to your goals then set a course of action, start now and remove the whole future-focused and completely inconsequential word *should* from your vocabulary. *Should* has no power because it always puts a future-pointed perspective on what we want to do. It has no real impact in creating positive actions.

If we feel that we should meditate we can instead say, "I meditate" and then set a course of action to do it. I could say, "I should write every day", but this presupposes that I *don't* write every day. More powerful ways to phrase my intention would be that "I write every day" or simply "I am an author".

Drop should – and just do what YOU want to do.

Passion and purpose are synonymous with a life well lived. When we act deliberately, we are taking accountability for our own actions. We are removing the possibility of victimising ourselves and blaming others. Acting deliberately involves making *powerful* decisions – decisions that we have taken full responsibility for. Acting deliberately means living life *on purpose!*

It is interesting to note that when we act deliberately, we also allow ourselves to surrender to what will be. If we dither and dally in our decisions, and if we resign ourselves to situations, or react to circumstances instead of acting in a forthright manner, we are more likely to worry about and cling to the results of those actions; however, when we act deliberately and with power and conviction we take accountability to the extent that surrender is a natural end result. We have acted in the only way that we can, in the moment, to take ourselves closer to our dreams, and because we have done so, whatever actually occurs will be in the hands of the universe/divine. In this way if the outcome is not what we hoped for or expected, we can act with the pragmatic assurance that there is learning in the process (often our failures and disappointments provide our greatest teachings), that there is a necessary karma that needs to be played out, and that we can continue to act deliberately and with assurance – *we* are in control of our actions and they help to *co-create* our reality in conjunction with the machinations of the universe.

IT'S YOUR LIFE: THE TRAP OF BEING 'CONVENTIONALLY UNCONVENTIONAL'

Your path is unique. Stepping outside the norm, if the norm isn't working for you, is going to look very different for everyone. Simply wearing more tie-dyed T-shirts, growing your hair long and slipping into sandals will not make you happier, and neither will dropping out of society, becoming a Buddhist or doing any of the other things listed on the blog 'Stuff White People Like' – unless of course those are the things that truly enrich your life, surround you with like-minded people and give you truly wonderful moments of experience … if not you're simply being conventional, but in different clothes.

"Man, the living creature, the creating individual, is always more important than any established style or system."
~ Bruce Lee

Remove *should*

For the next few days begin to be aware of how often you tell yourself that you *should* do something, and how often you say that you *should* do things when in conversation.

Think to yourself: *Who says that I should?*

Is this in fact justified? Do you feel that you should do things because they are expected by others or they fall into what is considered the norm?

Recognise which things you feel you should do because they fit in with what you want to do and who you want to be (for example, "I should eat healthy, organic, natural, unprocessed food") and change this into a positive mindset of wanting to do it, loving doing it or simply doing it, for example, I *love* eating healthy, organic, natural foods!

If there are things you feel that you should do because of others, think about whether you in fact even want to do those things – and if not, simply drop them and move on.

Would an unconventional action make your life better or easier?

Relax, breathe and allow yourself to become calm. Think about your life and your daily patterns and actions. Are there any things you could do, or have wanted to do, that are unconventional but would make your life easier or better?

Take a large piece of paper and with a pen, pencil, crayon or marker write these things down. Evaluate the pros and cons of these actions and think deeply about whether your fears are justified. Some of these actions may be things that you bring into your life and, whilst unconventional, could become part of your happiness 'toolbox'.

Reflections

Are my goals defined in only monetary terms, or do I make money to achieve my goals?

What have I been putting off and waiting for the 'right moment' to do?

Do I work for work's sake?

Am I living my life on purpose?

(If you answered 'no' to the last question, then start NOW!)

CHAPTER FOUR

Work, Live, Play

Becoming a 'Life Artist'

"WHAT WE REALLY *WANT* TO DO IS WHAT WE ARE REALLY MEANT TO DO. WHEN WE DO WHAT WE ARE MEANT TO DO, MONEY COMES TO US, DOORS OPEN FOR US, WE FEEL USEFUL, AND THE WORK WE DO FEELS LIKE PLAY TO US."
~ JULIA CAMERON

Sometimes I feel as if I have never worked a day in my life … and it's not because I am a 'trustafarian', born with a silver spoon in his mouth that doesn't need to work to make a living. In fact while my middle-class family were far from poor (my father, an electrician, and my mother, a teacher, worked their butts off to make sure that we had more than just the necessities), we certainly had our fair share of really lean times, and it was only because of their tireless efforts that we didn't fall well below the poverty line.

57

Nor is it because I'm too lazy to work or get stuck in and do hard work. In fact, an article by Emily Beers in the 'Performance Advocate' e-zine of November 2007 had this to say:

"Cliff Harvey is the kind of guy who makes people ask the question, 'What doesn't this guy do?' His credentials include being a nutritionist, a natural therapist, a strength coach, a philosopher, and a writer. Oh yeah, he is also a World Champion athlete … After just a brief interview with Harvey, it became apparent that he is indeed a rare breed - one of those unique individuals who enjoy having an overwhelming load on his plate. In fact, he takes the expression 'a lot on your plate' to a whole new level …"

I went on in the interview to say, "Being busy is often seen as a negative, but when you are working with great people, doing something you love, it can be so positive."

I don't quote this to be self-aggrandising, but merely to illustrate that I have worked as hard and as long as anyone over the years – in my naturopathic, health and strength practice and in my sporting life. In fact, I have often found myself working 12 and 13-hour (or longer) days –sometimes without even realising that I'm working! However, I *feel* as if I haven't worked a day in my life because I absolutely love what I do, and I approach my work with mindfulness and awareness. It is so very important to appreciate every moment of life, even if at times we feel as if we are 'stuck' doing something we don't want to do (which of course we aren't – whatever we do in life is a choice we have made.

I also choose regularly to take stock, step back and take the time to travel, to train, to read, write, eat great food and compete in the sports I love … in fact to do any of the myriad things I love to do.

Our Relationship With 'Work' Defines How We Feel About It

The idea of 'work' provides a lot of mental stress and anguish for many, but it is not working itself that provides stress to us – it is our relationship with our work situation that makes it stressful. We can change our relationship with our work situation in order to find the breaking moments of happiness that can be present in *any* job or vocation.

The approach that we take to our workday defines how we actually perceive it.

Sometimes I still dislike getting out of bed in the morning. I, like everyone else, occasionally get sick of the compulsion to work in order to make enough money to enjoy my time. But if I had all the money in the world, I think I would actually change very little. You see, I love my clients, I love helping them to enjoy greater health, greater performance and a greater quality of life. This is something that has become abundantly clear to me when I have taken extended breaks from work. I really begin to miss the interaction and the close personal relationships I have with my clients and colleagues. I also miss the ability to make a definitive difference in someone's life on a one-to-one level. I have certainly realised in periods away from my practice that one of my greatest life purposes – an integral part of my personal legend – is to be of service to others. And it's something I wouldn't give up for all the money in the world. In fact, this is one of the things that get me through those hard days when I wake up thinking: *Oh God, I don't want to do this today.* The idea that I can imbue someone's life with joy makes it that much easier to stump up and do what has to be done. I'm also fortunate that I have been able to shift my life to the point where my passions of writing and speaking take up a lot of my time and provide a significant portion of my income. This was a choice that I made. I made a decision to forgo some of the business and work activities that were providing financial stability in order to pursue what I most wanted to be doing (which was helping people through writing and lectures to live healthier, happier lives). It was not a resignation, nor a windfall that allowed this – instead my path was forged through a series of powerful decisions. But the decision alone to do something extraordinary doesn't necessarily provide us with the life purpose and satisfaction we would like, especially initially, and most evidently if we are building a new business or career from the ground up. At these times how we relate to our working day plays a major part in ensuring that we take enjoyment out of our days.

I think it is imperative that we all – each and every one of us – have some sort of purpose in life, and the work we do day to day is such a big part of that.

From a pragmatic point of view, if we are trying to maximally leverage our time, so that we may 'suck the marrow out of life' and enjoy our waking moments to the full, it would be a shame to waste so much of it doing things we don't enjoy – or more correctly *not enjoying the things we do*. This distinction is actually quite important. We can love what we do because we enjoy the sense of satisfaction and fulfilment it gives us. When we are very good at something and we are able to translate it into a career, it can be as if that's what we were put on this earth to do.

But what if we don't have this?

What if we don't know exactly what we want to be doing?

Many of my clients grapple with this. They don't always feel they are in the career or job situation that they want to be. But if they don't know yet what they want to really be doing, it can be extremely frustrating. However, in the absence of having discovered the alternative, we can still enjoy our jobs and enjoy our careers.

Every job, every position, every environment is unique, and there will, in almost all cases, be nuances that make it enjoyable. It could be the interaction with colleagues, challenging projects, worthwhile causes – all of these things can give us a reason to 'be' in any situation. I have found the personal interactions and relationships, in almost any situation I've been in, to be great motivators and also great sources of satisfaction. If, in any given situation, I can try and bring some warmth, kindness and compassion to another person, it is worth it. This can even be as simple an act as deciding, just as you hit a traffic jam, not to be angry and impatient but instead to see it as an opportunity to be kind and to slow down to let people merge (try it, it's such a release not to be worrying about the delays and inconvenience and instead to be focused on simply being kind).

You can also apply this to work and make a decision to be kind and bring a new level of empathy to your personal interactions.

It is our relationship with circumstances in our lives that creates frustration, disappointment or dissatisfaction – *not the circumstances themselves*. We co-create our reality, moment by moment, and we can choose to change our relationship with our work and with what we do on a day-to-day basis to bring joy to it. We can, in the absence of finding our dream job (which may be an ever-retreating mirage anyway), create 'dream interactions' with the world and people around us, thereby bringing joy into our lives.

Many people who have what they consider to be their dream jobs (I'm one of them) would actually be happy doing many different things. Most of the happiest, most relaxed people I know – people who have a passion for what they do, and live life *on purpose* – have a huge range of interests, hobbies and activities they engage in regularly. Given a life change, any of these activities could conceivably be what the person builds a career around. I have, for example, worked at various times and for various reasons (most usually for adventure and experience) as an electrician's labourer, a reprographic consultant, a bouncer, strength coach, nutritionist, naturopath, spiritual counsellor, author and motivational speaker. I enjoyed all these pursuits, and the reasons were that that they gave me a new and interesting experience and allowed me to interact with new and interesting people.

YOUR JOB IS A CONDUIT FOR YOUR LIFE'S PURPOSE

We can often get 'stuck' trying to imagine and find the 'perfect' job for us, a job that will provide the passion and drive to live a life of joy. But this really is putting the cart before the horse.

When we recognise the type of life we would like to be living, and the person we really want to be, we can see there are probably many occupations that meet those end goals, and in fact many of us can achieve exactly what we want in our self-growth and our interactions with others within our present occupation.

For example, if you want to be of service to others, if you want to give back to humanity, you could do this, and be very effective as a bus driver, a store keeper, a barman or a health practitioner – the list really is endless, and if you want to bring joy into your daily life, it begins and ends with *you*. By looking outside ourselves and expecting our career or the people around us to create happiness is completely futile. We must start with the intention of love and positivity, and this creates the burgeoning growth of love and positivity around us, which in turn can create the environment in which we want to exist.

I had a wonderful experience at a facility where I was consulting as a strength coach and nutritionist.

At this place there were a number of trainers, strength coaches and allied health practitioners. Most of them were pretty friendly and open, but one guy just seemed to avoid everybody. A few of the coaches I got to know well said he was unfriendly and even a little rude … but I wasn't so sure.

What was certainly true was that every time I walked past him, he looked away and didn't say a word to me.

Now, I could have fallen into line with the rest of the trainers and coaches and let it slide, assuming that was 'just the way he is' and avoid him as much as he avoided me and the others. But I didn't want to have that negativity in my environment. So instead I made a concerted effort to catch his eye every time we walked past one another and to smile and say hello. At first, he still avoided eye contact, and ignored me, but after a little while he started to hold eye contact just that bit longer and to say hello back. And within a short time, he began to smile and even to initiate conversation. And the reality is that he is a lovely guy. He wasn't being rude and obnoxious by not talking to people – *he was just really shy!*

I now look forward to seeing him, instead of it being a drag. Other people have noticed and have started doing the same and it now seems as if the whole place has had an 'energy lift' with people talking to those they didn't previously talk to, and there are more smiles and more 'good mornings'.

These small efforts that we make pay us back tenfold. I get a real kick out of my chats with this guy now, and he, after attending one of my lectures at a major fitness conference in Canada, gave me some of the most heartfelt and gratifying feedback I have ever received. What a shame it would have been if I had simply ignored him and missed out on getting to know a genuinely nice person.

The take-home message is to enjoy your work, or at the very least don't waste your time and your life while you are at work. Use it as an opportunity to learn, to grow, to live and to love. Use the interpersonal dynamics at work to make it worthwhile and positive, and if you *do* know the career that fits with *your* life of purpose then pursue it.

It is a waste of life to be doing something you don't want to be doing for five-sevenths of your waking time! *You* have the power to choose what *you* want to be doing and *you* are able to spend your 24 hours exactly as you wish.

Spend it doing something that makes you happy and be happy doing what you do!

Keep interested in your own career, however humble; it is a real possession in the changing fortunes of time.

~ From the Desiderata by Max Ehrmann

CREATING YOUR ART, EXPRESSING YOUR TRUTH

Living a life of joyous experience is not, I repeat, *not*, about working less. *It is about enjoying more.*

In the modern world many of us have lost the enjoyment from what we do because we have lost the element of craftsmanship in many trades.

We are beset with cheaply produced, mass-market consumer items, none of which involves the very human element of craftsmanship.

Craftsmanship is art, and art is the expression and creativity of pursuing that which you love. In the words of

Seth Godin: *'Doing The Work can do nothing else but create joy in your work.'*

I'm sure you've all heard these, or similar quotes spouted by business gurus:

> *'Are you working for your money? Or is your money working for you?'*
>
> *'If your business won't last without you there, you're not in business.'*
>
> *'Are you in business, or merely self-employed?'*

And I guess that if you're anything like me you've at least wondered at times about how you can turn your work into a business. But are these models even valid for the new paradigm?

They absolutely can be … **but they are not a necessity**. Having a richness of time is more important than simply having more time, particularly if you don't know what to do with your time. If you haven't allowed yourself to dream and dream big, you won't know what to do with your time! And in this scenario any additional amount of time – or money – will be worthless.

There are of course many people who are able to replicate what they provide in some way through products, certifications, books, DVDs, education systems – the list goes on. But there are many more who are content with being *great* practitioners of whatever it is that they do, *crafting* their products and services and affecting their clients profoundly on a day-to-day basis. Many in the business world look at this as a negative situation. The idea of being paid for time is seen as anathema as you always have to 'be' there in practice, and you are only paid for your time.

I can understand that perhaps if you make clothes pegs or high-tech widgets you may not necessarily want to be there all the time (unless of course you are a craftsman making really cool, funky clothes pegs) but if you love doing what you do, if it is your art and your expression, are you not in the enviable position of not needing to remove yourself from it? After all, we create happiness by spending our time on joyous experiences. Of course, we also need money as a conduit to achieve certain, but not all, of those joyous experiences and what we do in the work we love is a win-win situation of having a joyous experience – and being paid for it.

Being a tradesman is looked down upon in many circles, and being a businessman is lauded. But why is this? Have we lost the respect for the craftsman who plies his trade in the creation of things of superior quality? Is this because in our throwaway consumer culture, quality of goods and services is becoming an ever-rarer commodity?

I remember as a young personal trainer and nutritionist talking with an exercise physiologist friend of mine. He asked what I was currently up to, to which I replied, "Mainly doing nutrition. I still do a bit of training on the side."

One of my mentors – a very successful trainer – overheard this, took me aside and said, "Cliff, you don't do personal training 'on the side', you are *way* too good a trainer to put yourself down like that. What is wrong with being a *great* trainer?"

And you know what? There is absolutely nothing wrong with being great at anything, no matter what it is. If you love it, do it. And there certainly is nothing wrong with loving what you do and wanting to do it each and every day.

We seem to have lost the idea of craftsmanship and along with it the ideal of mastery, and while there are ample avenues available to replicate our skill sets through informational products, or create more highly leveraged income through other product sales, the fact remains that if we truly love being in practice and if we love what we do, why on earth would we want to get away from it?

The disparaging paradigm of being self-employed as not being good enough (à la Robert Kiyosaki and others) becomes moot when you aren't really working for your money but are involved in a process of making both yourself and someone else happier.

People often crave the freedom of having more time to themselves, only to realise when given more time that they have little to fill it with. This is a problem with not having found joyous experience in life, not one of not having enough time.

We see this in evidence when people retire. They often find – after years of toiling in unfulfilling careers – that when finally given the chance to sit back and relax and do some of the things they have always wanted to do, they are too tired and too sick to do it. Or they simply don't know what they should do with their time.

The goal is not to simply work less. The goal is to do more of what we love and what we enjoy in life. This is the real goal of creating a business 'of you, for you'.

People who are actively involved in the pursuit of their passion don't always have the financial option (not immediately anyway) or the inclination (because they love what they do) to severely minimise their work hours. But they do have the power to reduce the time cost of other extraneous things. The message, though, can become lost, so I'll re-iterate it.

We need not work less ~ we need to do more of what we love!

As I was growing up, my father always told me, "Cliff, I don't mind what you end up doing in life, just be the best!" He really did not care what I ended up as. If I were to be a street sweeper, he simply wanted me to be the best street sweeper I could be. If I were to be a lawyer, entrepreneur, billionaire, he simply wanted me to be the best that I could be.

In life so often we *are* our businesses anyway, and this to my mind is a positive, not a negative. We are re-entering an age of personality and interpersonal connection, rather than simply reducing the costs of production. There is, after all, only so much cheap crap we can buy and sell before we say enough's enough.

My clients are attracted to me for me, just as others are attracted to other authors and mentors. They want to receive health and spiritual coaching from me, and I want to spend time working with them. There are many other things I could be doing in life, but I choose to spend my days working with people, in person, in lectures and through my writings.

What we can do for the business of ourselves is to create mastery in what we do and to realise that our craft, our trade, is also our art. It's our expression, and by living our craft as well as we realistically can, we are facilitating the health and happiness of not just ourselves, but our clients and all those who come into contact with our work.

DOING 'THE WORK'

As mentioned earlier, I picked up the term 'the work' from Seth Godin's incredible book, *Linchpin*.

He uses the term 'the work' rather than simply 'work' to define creative or artistic endeavours — which anything that drives and provides for a passion and purpose in our life, can be. More than simply 'work', *THE* work is the endeavour of your passion. In essence it is the goal of your life's purpose, with other rewards being as a result of doing 'the work'.

Unlike 'work' that *needs* to be done in order to achieve something – being merely a means to an end, and often with little or no inherent value or reward – THE work is all an artist can do.

I remember a quote, perhaps from the memoirs of my favourite author Gabriel Garcia Marquez: '… that if a writer can**not** write, *then he's not a writer.*'

If not for the work, the artist ceases to be.

For the artist *the work* never ceases, for it is the impetus that drives a life worth living. There is no pot of gold at the end of the rainbow, nor a time when *the work* is done. For the artist, the craftsman, the artisan loves his work, and why would one seek to be without that which he loves?

The work is how the artist changes the world and brings joy to his fellow man. It is his contribution to the story of our lives.

We are all artists; we can all create, even if that creation is simply a little more joy and happiness. Your art may not be with paint on canvas, or words on paper, but if you have found *the work* that pulls you forward and compels your passion, that flows with joy and love, then *your* art, *your* work can be that which brings joy to your life, and is the change that changes the world.

When we realise that we are all artists of life we can begin to truly experience the integration of work, life and play.

Wealth v. 'Success'

Regardless of our own conscious views of what really constitutes a successful life, many of us will fall into the set point of thinking that success, by and large, is primarily measured monetarily. This is after all the prevailing paradigm. Think about some of the conversations you may have had in the past: "Oh yeah, he's a really *successful* guy but he just doesn't seem happy," or "Even with all her *success* she was never really happy."

Wow … really?

When we define success by one measure, we miss the importance of what success actually is. And sadly, we define ourselves further into a paradigm into which it is deemed to be crucial to be a 'success' in life, even when that success is defined by a measure that may not lead to any degree of lasting happiness, life fulfilment or satisfaction.

What is success?

Success: noun

1. the accomplishment of an aim or purpose: *the president had some* **success in** *restoring confidence*

2. the attainment of fame, wealth, or social status: *the success of his play*

3. [count noun] a person or thing that achieves desired aims or attains fame, wealth, etc.: *to judge from league tables, the school is a success.*[4]

The primary definition of success in other words is: The achievement of something desired, planned, or attempted and so success is predicated upon what *you* want to achieve, not what is considered to be the norm in society.

But does the definition of success truly denote what it really means to be successful?

The secondary definitions of success certainly show how synonymous the *ideas* of wealth and fame *have* become with success but we must consider that if you desire for and plan for material wealth, and in the achieving of this you don't find a measure of lasting happiness and a sense of life purpose and fulfilment, then is that indeed moot? Therefore, could you really say that you are a success?

To truly not just be considered a success against a societal benchmark, but to truly feel and truly *be* successful,

---

[4] Oxford Dictionary Online:
http://www.oxforddictionaries.com/definition/success?view=uk

you must measure your success against the measures of your own making.

When I wrote *Choosing You!* for example, I had immediate financial aspirations and goals for the book. When I first began to evaluate what would make the book a success, my conditioned mind immediately began jumping to profit and revenue and the sales that would need to occur to make this a reality.

Now there is nothing at all wrong with profit and revenue, except that it wasn't truly the best measure for *my* success.

I had many nagging doubts about releasing the book, due in part to a reticence to put myself 'out there' to criticism, but also in part because fundamentally if you realize that your measure of success is different to that of the prevailing world view, then you can become worried about whether people will understand, and, of course, that they will think you are a failure (i.e. *not* a success) if you don't reach *their* measure of success — even if you reach your own.

My friend and mentor, author Dr Ian Brooks, encouraged me to release the book for *me,* and be defined by my own measure of success; sage counsel that I was blessed to receive. I had to refocus and contemplate what success really means to me and by *that* measure decide what success for the book would truly be — for *me.* I decided that if just one person, somewhere in the world, was profoundly and positively affected by the book then I would consider it a success.

I reached this simple, yet powerful goal when I received my first unsolicited testimonial from a woman in South Africa. There have since been many testimonials like that, and although I couldn't retire off the proceeds of the book sales nor live in the lap of luxury because of the royalties, the exercise was *for me* a success according to *my rules*.

You need not be a rock star!

IF you *love* what you do, and if you find a passion and a purpose in your work, you are an artist. And anyone *can* be an artist. In fact one of the areas I work on with my clients is recovering the artistry and creativity in what they do in order to live a life of greater purpose and satisfaction. Becoming an artist (in whatever you do) is a way to not only enjoy life more, but to future-proof yourself as well.

If you are simply a 'piece of the machine' providing services or products that are procedure based, you may be replaced very easily with a machine or with a lower cost human alternative. But if you are an artist – someone who brings creativity, customisation and craftsmanship to what you do – you take yourself out of the crowd and become a unique identity; and a unique identity can't be replaced.

Sometimes doing what we love, and doing things that bring joy to us and others, can be seen as frivolous. There is an idea that 'real work' is doing something that is stable and secure, and that gets paid in a steady, ongoing manner. We are constantly told to 'get a real job', 'stop chasing dreams' and – my favourite – 'grow up'. This is even true when we are working *really* hard to make a success of our artistic endeavours.

I have been lucky enough to spend a lot of time with – and for periods live and work with – several friends who are musicians, actors and designers. All of them to a person are incredibly hard-working and spend their valuable time honing their craft, doing 'the work' and spreading the word about what they are doing.

It can be a long and arduous process, but one none of them would give up because they absolutely love it with a passion.

I have spent countless nights with these folks, working on projects and at performances, screenings and showings, and I can tell you it ain't easy. And in spite of this it is still seen as frivolous, and perhaps that is due not just to a perception that it's not 'real work' but because it is so hard to achieve fame and fortune for the vast majority of people plying their artistic craft; however, we fall into a trap when we see the options available to an artist as only hyper-success or failure.

In fact you need not become a rock star.

There are many viable ways in which to ply your trade, do the work and be an artist and have it pay the bills (well), without also having to have extraordinary levels of fame.

Of course those who do achieve fame are considered exceptions to the rule, and their level of success is seen as a justification for their existence as artists. In other words, it is not always acceptable to be an artist unless you are successful. This is a ridiculous circular argument, as one cannot become a successful artist without putting in the hard work of being an artist first!

The modern world has many opportunities for artists to become micro-celebrities, where their art (in whatever form it takes), is taken up and appreciated by a small sector of committed fans, and this can be a viable way for an artist in the new economy to live by their trade. But even when artists are doing what they love, are affecting people's lives and making a good living from their art, it is almost as if they are still not successful due to their lack of rock-star status.

It's really funny how a micro-celebrity, musician or author, for example, can be derided by people saying, "I've never heard of him"; but if you were to mention your lawyer, particularly to someone outside your city, it is doubtful whether anyone would have heard of him either. Oh, but he has a 'real' job. (Notwithstanding the he or she might also be an 'artist' of law, or even a veritable 'rock star' in legal circles).

I was recently talking to a supposed music industry aficionado about several up-and-coming bands. She made an offhand comment that their sales were 'nothing' in spite of the fact that several of these bands are living quite comfortably off the proceeds of their albums, along with touring and merchandise and are cultivating their most loyal followers into long-term, die-hard fans. Their sales may be considered 'nothing' in contrast to the sales of Metallica, ACDC or U2, but those same sales are providing a comfortable living to the artists and supporting wonderful art that is appreciated by thousands of people. That most definitely is not 'nothing', and in fact we need more of that style of enterprise in the world.

In reality they are working along the lines of the '1000 True Fans' model coined by Kevin Kelly[5] and popularized by Seth Godin, except it's more like tens of thousands of true fans in these cases.

That they are making a living as artists and loving doing it is the most important aspect to me, and artists, too, need to get rid of the outdated notion that they should either be stellar, multi-million selling mega-rich rock stars, or get out of the biz. It is not 'all or nothing', as the craft itself is the process, and the process (*'the work'*) if we love it, should be reward enough – assuming we are in fact making enough to live. If we *aren't* making enough to live,

---

[5] http://www.kk.org/thetechnium/archives/2008/03/1000_true_fans.php

then maybe our craft will not be our 'job' but it most certainly can still be our passion.

The work required to sell millions of copies of a book or an album, or become known as a painter may not be any different from selling hundreds, or thousands, and the talent required to be the most famous won't necessarily make one so. It is essential to success, but it does not make success a surety.

I had a brief discussion online with my great friend, the gifted healing practitioner Marielle Smith, about 'when' someone decides to call themselves a writer, author or musician. There seems to be a reticence to call oneself an artist until an arbitrary and unrealistic level of success is achieved. For a long time, I would refer to myself as an 'aspiring' writer, in spite of being published in magazines on three continents and affecting the lives of many thousands through these articles and through my first book, *Choosing You!*

But I got over it.

I'll reiterate that it is not to say that the financial rewards of our labours are not important – they are; however, they most certainly are no more important than the achievement of a more lasting sense of purpose, direction, fulfilment and happiness – and these are not always synonymous with the accrual of monetary reward for our work. I need to eat and put a roof over my head just as you do, and it must be said that I was proud of the sales of my first book, but the achievement of gross levels of wealth is not a factor in determining my success. Creating a positive impact on the world and helping people to live happier, healthier lives takes precedence over the abject pursuit of material wealth. That, more than anything, defines what I consider to be a successful life for me. To see someone smiling where before there was a frown. To have someone leave my office pain-free after a life of debilitating hurt means more than any amount of money.

That is my life of success. What is yours?

What would you MOST *love* to do?

Stop, breath and relax. Spend a few moments simply noticing your breathing and allow yourself to settle into a state of calmness.

Ask yourself, "What would I MOST like to do for a career or vocation?"

Be completely open to any suggestions or thoughts that arise. Remember – this is *your* time to dream!

Take a large sheet of paper and write down any ideas you have. Continue writing things down until you hit a 'wall' with your thought process.

Look at the things you have written down.

- Could any of these be a potential career for you?

- If not, could they be a hobby that you could be passionate about?

- Do any (or most, or all) of these contain elements that you could bring into your life and career *right now* without necessarily having to change what you do?

Create connections in the workplace

For at least one week focus on creating only positive, loving and compassionate relationships with everyone in your workplace – *especially* the most annoying ones!

Use an affirmation such as: "Every one of my relationships rewards and enriches my life" and repeat it to yourself often. You'll be surprised how much your intention to be open, loving and compassionate affects your day-to-day happiness.

1.   Refrain from gossiping about others – in fact, if you wouldn't say something in front of the person then don't say it at all.

2.   Smile, and say hello to everyone you see and pass when you get to your place of work.

Reflections

How do I define success – for me?

Do I enjoy going to work each day?

What things do I most want to get out of my work life?

Do I set my work–life goals around what I most want or around an arbitrary wage or salary amount?

Dream Big

How to set the goals that really matter

"GOD GIVES US DREAMS A SIZE TOO BIG SO
THAT WE CAN GROW INTO THEM."
~ AUTHOR UNKNOWN

Setting goals is crucial for achieving what we want in life. Unfortunately, most people get goal setting all wrong.

Sure, they set goals, and many of them even *achieve* their goals, but they may not have set goals that matter.

Those that really matter are those that put us closer to the life we really want to be living.

Goals provide direction. They are not in and of themselves the 'ultimate goal'. The ultimate goal is to be living a healthier, happier, more fulfilled life. In the pursuit of our goals our ultimate achievement can be to be completely involved in the 'process', which leads ultimately to a life of greater freedom and fulfilment. This provides a totality and completeness to our life which is encapsulated in the timeless wisdom of 'being here now' – a theme we see in all the major contemplative traditions.

In order to actually set the goals that matter, we need to begin with a general exploration of what we really want to be doing in life, as defined by the type of life we want to be living and the type of person we really want to be. This provides a 'best-case' scenario of what life could be, thereby providing the fertile ground for setting the right goals within the right context.

Without having that context, we really are flying blind. If we set goals without having first explored the greater issue of 'where is this all leading me?' we are merely clutching at straws in the hope of gaining some life direction … even if that life direction is not leading us where we want to go.

Without having a context for the type of person we want to be and the type of life we want to lead, we cannot use our time effectively doing things that will give us the greatest amount of joy and satisfaction.

It is our highest aspirations that define the goals we need to be setting. When we have an idea of what the best-case scenario might look like, we can strive to achieve goals that help to make it a reality.

'Try' not. Do or do not. There is no 'try'.
~Master Yoda

Living Life on Purpose

Many of us get stuck in the trap of thinking that we simply 'are who we are'; that we are a certain type of person, and that we behave and act according to this. But this thinking is fundamentally flawed. Who we are does not happen by accident. We are who we ourselves have created over the course of our lifetime; through the succession of choices we make.

It is true that what we are exposed to has a definite effect on us. We are conditioned, to a large degree, by the sum of all the experiences we have had over our lifetime. But we have free will and inclination, and if we so choose, we can decide to act in response to situations instead of merely reacting to them according to our conditioning. Because of this we can create who we are and who we will be! But of course, we need to know the type of person we want to be and the life that we want to be living in order to act in a way that will take us closer to that.

When we have a better idea of *who* we want to be, we can also know what experiences and achievements will make that a reality and, in turn know what we will need to have as the tools of those experiences.

1.   Know who you want to be

2.   Know what you want to do and achieve

3.   Know what you want to have

Note: Knowing what you want to *have* is a result of knowing who you want to be and what you want to achieve, as possessions should be tools by which you achieve experience – they are not the goal itself.

1.   Know who you want to be

"Who do you want to be?"

The person that you are defines what you do, therefore the person that you want to be provides the context for what you need to do, what you want to achieve and by extension what you want to *have*.

2.   Know what you want to do and achieve

"What do you want to do and achieve?"

In the context of knowing the type of person you want to be and the way you want to live your life, there will be innumerable *experiences* that you want to have as part of that life.

Experiences provide the moments of growth, joy and fun that we are able to indulge in as a result of spending our time on the things most important to us, and they in turn enrich our time. To maximally achieve this, we need to know what we are going to spend our time on and prioritise what is going to give us the greatest benefit and enjoyment for our time expenditure.

Positive, joyful experiences are innumerable and are bounded only by what you want to do, the person you are now, the person you *want* to be, and most importantly, by your imagination! The things that you want to do and achieve could, for example, be travelling, learning a new language, learning to dance, taking up a new sport or martial art, skydiving … in fact anything you can think of that drives your passion and purpose to live a life worth living.

Don't be afraid to write your personal legend on the

pages of your life's book!

3.   Knowing what you want to have

"What do you want to have?"

Possessions are much less of a concern for the time rich than experiences. But let me say this loud and clear …

There is nothing at all wrong with having possessions, and with wanting and enjoying the material things in life.

Why, after all, would we seek deliberate hermeticism?

People with abundance and richness of time are not fanatics; in fact, I consider the ideal of the time rich to be an extremely pragmatic one. Material possessions and wealth are not 'bad'.

It is all too easy to vilify wealth and those who have it, but we need not get stuck in this trap. Looking enviously at others is one thing and one thing only: *A waste of time.* It's an ego trap that only serves to sap our time and energy. And as we know, time is our most important currency – why spend it envying what others have? At the end of the day it is not what people 'have' that allows them to enjoy their time, but what they 'do'.

And so, what we seek to *have* should be defined by *what we want to do*. Possessions are the tools of experience.

Consider this example: If you have always wanted to buy a Ferrari because you are a passionate driver and love engines, fast cars and the feeling of luxury that comes from a fine automobile, then that is a great reason to buy one; however, if you want to buy a Ferrari because it will enhance your social status or because it will show that you are wealthy (or at least have the appearance of wealth … the two are not the same!) I would not consider that a good reason. To work towards something for purely extrinsic motivation is a low personal reward strategy, and it can be a double-edged sword. Many people amass the symbols of wealth and status to attract people into their lives, be they friends or romantic partners. But when we attract people by what we have, and not who we are, those relationships will always be fundamentally flawed.

Those who truly appreciate us and want to be with us, will be with us regardless (and often in spite of) the things we have.

Relationships are fundamentally rooted in time.

Q. What is the greatest thing you can provide for someone you love?

A. TIME!

Working towards things that are motivated by *intrinsic* factors always provides for greater and deeper satisfaction, and therefore has a high personal reward.

Possessions or achievements with a higher *extrinsic* motivation provide less satisfaction, which is of a much shorter duration.

The greater the level of intrinsic motivation, the higher the level of personal reward.

The old adage that 'if you always do what you've always done, you'll always get what you've always got' rings very true.

To live with a richness of time (joyous moments) and an abundance of time we need to know fundamentally the type of life we'd like to be living, and this, more than anything else, requires us to know the type of person we want to be. Quite literally we need to have an overlying philosophy of *who* we want to be.

Defining the person we want to be does require some action. The *absence* of a specific decision and a specific resolution to do something, quite obviously means nothing will occur.

91

Defining Your Dreams

In various mind–body disciplines it is common to hear the term 'dream-setting'. This is subtly but crucially different to what one might usually consider goal setting.

Dream-setting defines what we want to achieve, not in terms of our consciousness, but it is subconscious in nature and in line with our *highest good*.

The key 'take-home' point with this style of goal setting is not to 'set goals' but to 'set the goals that matter'.

This step is critically entwined with the idea of *'knowing who you want to be'* earlier in the chapter.

Many of us find it hard to put this into any sort of real context, and it may seem somewhat daunting, especially when we are often conditioned to believe that we are who we are by virtue of our genes and our upbringing, and that by the time we are adults we are more or less stuck with 'our lot' in life. But we aren't. Our lives are a constantly evolving, fluid process of our own creation. Not only can we change, but we can begin to do it now, and we *can* dream of a better life for us, and through action begin to make those dreams a reality.

The concepts that begin to emerge when we really look at who we want to be (our highest self) and how we want to be living (living to our highest potential) contain many of the nuances of what would be considered a good, moral, ethical life. Few amongst us on any sort of deep level want to be greedy, or narcissistic or hurtful; these only come out of weakness. That weakness is born of insecurity and a poor sense of self-worth that drives the ego to seek out power over others. When we have a better grounding of what *really* constitutes a good life, a life worth living (really living!), these negative aspects of 'being' simply fall away under the gaze of greater mindfulness and critical awareness.

There are subtle nuances, though, in the type of life that people would like to live, which is shaped by our passions, what we enjoy doing and what drives our creativity the most.

Encapsulating in Words the Life You Want to Live

Often, we can begin to sum up at least a large part of who we want to be in a few simple words. For example, if you simply let your mind go and think about what you most fundamentally would like to be, you might say: "I would like to be a happy, confident, honest person"

These words and ideas may at first seem a little unspecific and vague, but they are in fact remarkably powerful indicators and guides for the life we want to be living. Rather than pushing them into the background because they are not as 'concrete' as more quantifiable goals and objectives, they should be used as a guiding premise for the formulation of goals and objectives. These simple words encapsulate a personal ideology and philosophy of being, without which our goals and objectives have no real purpose.

Words also provide the most common 'frame' which we wrap around concepts, feelings and emotions. Frames, whilst being incomplete and imperfect, are still powerful as a way to relate to events and situations and to provide a rational context for the universe around us.

A few choice and simple words can become a 'personal mantra'. If we say things to ourselves, they will begin, bit by bit, to come true. This is the value of positive 'self-talk'. By saying we *are* a certain way, or that we *have* certain faculties and abilities, we begin to believe it … but more importantly we begin to act in ways that make it a reality and by saying, believing and doing, we make real physiological changes to our brain and our neurochemistry in accordance with those thoughts.

As with words, we create images, metaphors and motifs around the various concepts of life, and these too can help create the preparation for the life we want to live.

We also have ideas on how we would like to be living our lives, what we would most like to be doing, the partner we would like to have and more. These things all provide context for our goals. If we can visualise the life we want to be living, we can begin to live it – *right now.* The power of visualisation in this respect cannot be underestimated. If we haven't thought about the person we want to be, we will not be able to act in ways that will make it a reality.

The ideas we have of the person we want to be can become a personal philosophy that provides the context for our own personal journey, with goals serving as waypoints along the path.

DREAM-SETTING IN PRACTICE

Dream-setting involves goal setting and time and financial budgeting for relatively short periods of time. I recommend no longer than 12 months at a time for the majority of my clients (most of whom are not doing *any* goal-setting work when we begin working together), and in fact most dream-setting can be honed down to even shorter time frames (three or six months works well.)

The key with this type of goal setting is to live in 'the now' and achieve goals and objectives within shorter time frames, no longer ones. Short time frames force us to re-evaluate our lives and our life direction more quickly, because the shorter the amount of time we have to do it the more quickly we will complete it.

Many goal-setting paradigms are based around long-term strategic planning and whilst this *can* be valuable, by its very nature, longer term goal setting is also more ambiguous. We cannot, no matter how concise we are with our planning, know all the obstacles, pitfalls (and windfalls!) that may beset us and cross our path between now and then, and the longer that goal's time frame, the more apparent this is. So, whilst longer term planning can help to encapsulate the type of life we want to be living, and holds value in this, shorter term goal setting is more valuable for actually progressing towards our life of greatest happiness and worth.

In this way we can see long-term goal setting as strategic, with short-term dream-setting/goal setting being more of a tactical exercise. Strategy is more theoretical, and with a major theme of this book being 'action' we shall focus on the tactical.

Parkinson's Law states: 'Work expands so as to fill the time available for its completion.'

In practice when we have a shorter time frame to accomplish something, we will work harder, more productively and more efficiently.

Goal setting and planning carried out too far in advance doesn't make us 'time accountable' enough to quickly achieve many of the things we want to achieve, and it also is more likely to need constant revisiting and adjustment as unexpected factors change the variables affecting the plan.

Chapter 5 Exercises

Visualisation: The best- and worst-case life scenario

A great way to connect to the life we want to live is to visualise the two extremes of what our perfect or best-case life would be, as compared to our absolute worst-case scenario.

Example meditation/visualisation

Start by relaxing in stillness and bringing yourself to your calm centre (if you are struggling with centring use the 'Mindfulness of Breath Meditation' in the exercises section of chapter eight).

When you feel calm, relaxed and at ease and are in a state of loving non-judgment, begin to imagine the absolute worst way you could be living your life. Think of where you would most like *not* to live, what is absolutely the worst job you could imagine and the worst types of relationships you could experience. Sit with and investigate this scenario in your mind's eye until you have a clear picture of it. Let this be a spontaneous projection from your subconscious – whatever comes up, comes up. Simply sit with this and build a vision of all the permutations: how you look and feel, what is going on around you, where you are, what you are doing and, overall, what you really are experiencing on a 'gut' level.

What themes and patterns define this scenario for you?

Does your current life hold aspects of this worst-case scenario that you could release?

Release any negativity, stress and anxiety and go back to a sitting meditation where you are able to observe any reactions to this visualisation in a loving, non-judging and compassionate way.

Repeat the process, except now imagine the absolute best-case life for you.

In this you may be surrounded by friends or loved ones and you will undoubtedly be doing something that you love.

What themes and patterns define this scenario for you?

Does your current life hold aspects of this best-case scenario already?

What things do you need to attract, or build into your life, that would make this scenario a reality?

In the same way you did with the previous worst-case scenario, again release the attachment, (even though positive) by re-entering a Mindfulness of Breath meditation.

Remember that releasing the positive (that is, not becoming overly attached to the outcome of 'happiness') is also a valuable exercise in learning that everything, be it positive or negative, eventually ends and we should be engaged in a process, not attached to outcomes.

Another great way to perform this visualisation is to imagine the best case for both living and dying.

The most common fear that people hold is the fear of death (perhaps superseded only by the fear of public speaking!). And whilst the seemingly complete indeterminacy of death is a daunting concept, by the same token the absolute certainty of death makes the fear of it limiting.

A common theme in spiritual traditions is the ability to connect with and, most importantly, accept death. By surrendering to death, we accept without reservation its inevitability, and by extension we are able to live more fully in the present, knowing that this life may end at any given moment. *By coming to peace with death we are able to live more fully.*

Several spiritual traditions, most notably in Tibetan Buddhism, have formulated exercises and rituals that allow people to accept and come to peace with death, both at the moment of death and in this life. (Sogyal Rinpoche explains this beautifully in his classic *The Tibetan Book of Living and Dying*.)

I strongly suggest (if you have access to a practitioner) going through a guided process known as a 'Life Bonding Balance' with an advanced-level Psych-K® practitioner.

This exercise takes you through the process of life in a style of guided meditation/visualisation from conception, through birth, into life, and finishing with a worst- and best-case death scenario, whilst also allowing a 'release' of trauma and anxiety associated with these events. (Check my website www.cliffharvey.com for my availability or www.psych-k.com to find a practitioner in your area.)

The greatest value in this exercise is that by tapping into our psyche and imagining our very worst-and best-case death scenarios, it illustrates quite vividly how we should be living our lives, and how we should not be living. It helps to highlight and illuminate the things that make us most happy and least happy – what we are prepared to accept and not accept in our best-case life.

I remember the first time I did this exercise I was slightly surprised by what my best-case and worst-case death scenarios were. When we are in a deep state of relaxation, and more open to signals from our deep subconscious, we can get signals of what really is most fundamentally important to us.

My worst-case death scenario involved me being frail and sick. It felt like I was suffering with lung cancer and was a shell of my former self. I felt like I hadn't achieved what I had wanted in life and that I hadn't helped to make the world a better place. Most evident was a feeling of being alone. Not only was I physically alone, but there was an all-pervading sense of not being loved, and not having anyone to love. I was cold, alone, damp, sick and miserable.

In contrast, my best-case death scenario involved me living in a simple hut on the beach. It was warm and peaceful in the afternoon sunlight, and I was sitting outside on the porch, overlooking the waves and feeling a deep sense of serenity. I KNEW that even though I was by myself at that moment, I was loved, and I had people that I too loved. I had a deep and true sense that I had lived a life worth living, and I had accomplished what I had been put on this earth to do and had left it a better place than when I entered. I was able to drift easily into the light and let go of this life with gratitude and enter the next transition with ease.

On reflection, after this meditation it really reminded me of the things that were most important to me: physical health, mental and emotional wellness, giving love, being in a physical environment that I loved and, most importantly, being of service to others and the world we live in.

How we would like to die can show us exactly how we should live.

The dream-setting process

Start by writing down a large goal.

This could be as simple as actually putting down on paper the type of life you want to be living.

Don't be afraid to think big and put down some BIG concepts on paper – you will hone these big concepts down to concrete objectives with this exercise.

Under this write down all the things you will need to do or have in order to reach this goal. Each one of these then becomes a topic itself and under each you can continue to write specific actions you need to take to achieve each step in the chain.

When you have honed down your biggest goals and dreams to tasks that can be done immediately, you have completed, for now – it can evolve – your initial dream-setting sheet.

When you have a set of specific actions and events that need to occur:

1. Choose a time frame (start with six months)

2. Write down all the things you want to do and achieve within this time frame.

3. Next to this list, write in an estimation of how much each of these will cost (many experiential things cost less a lot less than you might think.)

4. Write down all the things you want to 'have' in the next six months.

5. Next to this write down how much each of these will cost.

6. When you have done this, total up your lists.

Now split this up into either a daily or weekly breakdown and round up to the nearest $100 for weekly, or $10 for daily, totals.

This is how much you will have to earn over and above your day-to-day expenses to achieve your dreams and desires over the next six months.

The next step of course is to add up all your day-to-day cost of living. This is your budget. Align this with your dream-set and you will have a real figure for how much you need to earn in order to do the things that you want to do.

**Sample dream-setting sheets, goal-setting tools and
sample budget sheets available at
www.timerichcashoptional.com**

When you are drawing up a budget think of all the things you regularly spend money on. Make a mental inventory as you go through – if you see things that are inconsequential then cut them out and don't spend any more money on them. If there are items in your current expense list that are not enhancing your life, take them out of your budget.

There are many times in life when we fall into negative spending habits … just as we fall into other negative habits and behaviours in life. Often, we buy things, or begin to get into the habit of buying things, because we are trying to find some extra happiness or fulfilment in life. But as we have discovered, buying things without purpose is, at best, a pale substitute for buying the things that act as the tools for our joyous moments and experiences in life. Cutting out useless expenditure accomplishes two things: It allows us not to have to work as much to live the life we want to be living, and/or it allows us instead to spend money on things that we have identified will help to enrich our time.

Why waste money on the inconsequential, when instead you can spend it on things which enhance your valuable (and scarce) time?

What you spend your discretionary money on is completely up to you, and no one can tell you what you should and shouldn't cut back on … because you already know.

There are many things that are just not that important.

For example, I began writing this book whilst sitting on the couch in my apartment in Vancouver BC – where I was based for around three years. Previous to that I had been truly vagabonding (travelling and writing my way around South America, New Zealand and Canada) for about two years, and in five years I had only spent six months in total at home in Auckland, New Zealand.

Being away and not 'working' for two of those five years certainly created a laser focus for my spending, and, as a consequence, then – as now – I am spending very little on things outside of experiences. My priorities are great food and drinks with friends, travel, reading and sports I am actively involved in (and I am certainly not skimping on those things!). I have a roof over my head, clothes on my back, great food in my belly, and all my other basic needs are met. If I had fallen into the trap of seeing consumer goods advertised and thinking 'Wow! I could do so many cool things with Gadget X' and getting tied into finance payments or maintenance costs, I may not have been able to travel as much, see as much and experience so many wonderful sights, sounds and people as I have.

When we fall into the consumer spending trap, in reality we are creating a fantasy filled with 'things' that don't meet a real and true need.

Remember that possessions are the tools to reach the goal of positive experiences, not the goal itself.

Your dreams and goals day to day

Once you know how much you have to earn in order to achieve your short-term goals, you must make sure you are in fact earning enough to do it, or at least have enough surplus to make your dreams a reality. This may involve cutting back on inconsequential areas of spending to allow the discretionary income to do what you want it to be doing.

Or it may involve supplementing your income, getting a new job or taking up a new career path. Always allow a reserve of money to deal with unexpected and unforeseen costs. The amount of money you keep in reserve should be able to cover most unforeseen medical or transport costs (like having to buy a new car). A good figure to shoot for is to always have three to six months' worth of income in savings *at all times*.

Once you have your reserve and enough money to start doing the things on your list … start. Don't leave everything to the end of your dream line!

You have set a budget and a time frame in order to do the things that you want to do *within* that time frame. Set your plan, know your budget and start to live the life you want to be living now! Remember that we are not living a deferred life plan – we are living our lives on purpose, and we are living the lives that we want to be living … starting now!

Reflections

What type of life do I want to be living?

How do I want to treat people and how do I want to be treated?

What do I really want to do and achieve?

What do I need to 'have' to make these things a reality?

The Art of Satisficing

Simplifying your way to happiness

"OUR LIFE IS FRITTERED AWAY BY DETAIL
... SIMPLIFY, SIMPLIFY."
~ HENRY DAVID THOREAU

Simplicity, in a very real sense, can bring freedom. Simplifying our lives provides several key benefits:

- Reduced clutter

Physical clutter breeds mental clutter, and the less we have, the less we worry about having to keep track of all we have. This in turn reduces our mental stress significantly. Why do you think that tidying things up so that you know everything's place makes you feel mentally relaxed?

It's because you were trying — every time you saw a pile of mess or things out of place — to mentally decide *where* that should go and *when* you could conceivably organise things. Once it is all sorted out that (negative) mental stimulus is gone!

By having less to organise you immediately begin to free yourself from a lot of mental burden. It is important to realise what things are really crucial to living the life you want to live (this comes from your goal setting and dream-setting exercises) and get rid of the rest!

- Reduced expenditure of money

Requiring less obviously means we have to spend less to achieve our goals. We also gain more to spend on the important things (which are often experiential rather than physical) when we reduce our expenditure on the inconsequential things, which are often material possessions that are *not* tools of experience.

- Reduced expenditure of time

By not requiring as much, and not bringing as much into our lives, we do not have to work as much to service our daily lifestyle. There are less up-front costs of purchasing and less ongoing maintenance and upkeep costs – both of which are financial and time costs. By simplifying we reduce our time expenditure as well.

- Reduced requirement for space

Less 'stuff' requires less storage and space. This can serve a valuable end for someone who wants to live a life of experience, as it can further reduce the cost requirements and storage, for example, in the case of travel.

Simplify as much as possible because simplicity brings freedom.

What each of us views as simplicity, and how each of us live a 'simple' life, is different depending on our own values, wants and needs. But common to all of us is that we shouldn't overcomplicate things, for the simple reason that *complication expends too many resources*. Think about it this way. The less we have the fewer responsibilities we have. Therefore, with a more simple, minimalist lifestyle we are freed from devoting as much time and energy to responsibilities we would otherwise have. We need to weigh up the cost (in time and money) of the things we have and do and evaluate whether it is worth the time and energy to both *attract* and *maintain*.

Minimalism is not ascetism. Minimalism in the context in which we will explore it, is not simply about having less, and it is not about having less to attempt to 'tame the mind', or 'tame the spirit'. In fact, all of these concepts are quite inconsequential.

Minimalism in our paradigm is simply removing the inconsequential things in our lives so that we have more money and more time to devote to things that are most important to us. It is a rational and logical decision-making strategy to help us to get the absolute most out of our lives. In that way it allows us the 'biggest bang for buck'. Given that we have already begun to really evaluate what is most important to us, and what really drives the life of our dreams, the process of reducing clutter, removing the inconsequential and living in our own unique, minimalist way begins to become more and more a process of ease. It is not a process of deprivation, but instead a process that allows abundance, but it is an abundance of the things that matter.

Quite simply, we cannot ever have an abundance of *everything*! In fact it is irrational to expect to have an abundance of everything we can think of, because if it is not important to the life of our dreams, and therefore inconsequential, it is both a waste of time and money, and it is unethical as it becomes a wanton waste of resources.

Satisficing is a decision-making strategy that seeks a course of action that is 'good enough' but not necessarily perfect.

In life it is prudent to *strive* for perfection – but in striving for perfection we must also realise that we will never achieve it. Nothing in life is perfect; however, in striving for perfection we are seeking to do things to the best of our ability. The paradox is that in seeking perfection we achieve excellence, but perfection itself we simply cannot achieve.

In my practice I have noticed that what we would consider 'perfectionist' tendencies drive a huge amount of stress and anxiety in people. It is also a very powerful trait, as it often compels people to work to a level that is extraordinary, and those with perfectionist tendencies achieve to a level that many others do not. However, if someone is a perfectionist the danger is that they are *only* happy with the achievement of a 'perfect' result, and as perfection is an ever-retreating mirage, they will always have the anxiety of not having done their best, and their best not being good enough. An interesting side note is that when they drop the need for perfection and begin to believe that (in a practicable sense) they 'do their best, and their best *is* good enough' they still continue to work just as hard towards perfection, but the reality that perfection will not be achieved allows them to properly appreciate their achievements and reach greater levels of calm and peace day to day.

My best friend and his brothers are in what I consider to be one of the best rock bands in the world – *Like A Storm* (www.myspace.com/likeastorm.com). He was telling me once over a quiet beer how their latest recording efforts had been going. The band and the producer and engineer had been honing some of their latest songs. Initially they had really improved the songs and as they worked on them, they were becoming happier with them. But there came a point, he said, when the songs stopped becoming 'better' and were merely becoming 'different'.

It seems that in anything we do, there inevitably comes a time when we have to accept that it is 'good enough'

They had to decide to satisfice at this stage and realise – and accept – that they had done a great job on some kick-ass songs and move on to other tasks that were a more productive use of their time.

There comes a point when you are no longer improving something by continuing to work on it, but merely changing it.

Much of the concept of satisficing can be encapsulated by the simple formula of return on investment. We usually associate this with the financial return on a monetary investment; however, in the context of becoming time rich, we are looking at the amount of benefit, enjoyment and various other rewards we will get from something, as compared to the amount of time we put into it.

Here is an example from my own life:

I had always wanted to learn some form of dancing. I never really had any desire to dance per se, but I had always thought it was something a 'gentleman' should know how to do – perhaps I had watched too many James Bond movies or had heard too many stories about my Uncle Jim, a sailor, raconteur and ladies' man, and had a fantasy of me in a tux sweeping beautiful women off their feet. Either way, I wanted to learn how to dance!

I began to learn how to salsa, meringue and forréo from a dear friend of mine, a fantastic dance teacher, and to my surprise I really enjoyed it. Before I knew it, I was taking private lessons, learning steps really quickly and getting to a level of dancing proficiency bordering on advanced. But then my progress seemed to come to a halt. I had reached that mark where I had learned to perhaps an 80 per cent level of proficiency. I was a pretty good dancer, but was not yet, by any stretch of the imagination, a great dancer.

At this stage I didn't want to continue learning and putting in all the additional tuition time to improve only slightly over a long period. I just wanted to have some fun dancing with beautiful women! At the same time, I was also lifting weights competitively. I had reached a level of proficiency and had done well in some strength events. I guess

I was already at the stage of being 80 per cent proficient in this as well. Had this been purely a recreational activity I may have evaluated this and thought 'Hey, why would I want to put all these extra hours into lifting when I'm already stronger and a better lifter than most guys out there?' But the reality is that being 80 per cent good at something doesn't win medals or set records. To be the best, the very best, you have to sacrifice a disproportionate amount of time to go from 'good' to 'great'.

And so, in this instance, weightlifting, I made the decision to work disproportionately hard to go from a good level of proficiency to much higher, even though it took more work, time and effort to get that last 10 to 20 per cent than did the original 80 per cent.

The return on my time investment in this respect was that I won two world titles in All-Round weightlifting and set several world records, something I had strived for, had dreamed of, and had set as a goal to achieve. I was and still am proud of that achievement and also of the work it took to get there. Taking the easy road is not always the best for our continued growth and development, and of course achieving the really big goals never is easy!

However, becoming a better dancer than I already was would not have increased my enjoyment when I was out dancing anywhere near enough to justify the extra hours and work that would have been needed to increase my proficiency.

This encapsulates the idea of something we often hear referred to as the '80:20' rule, otherwise known as Pareto's Law. This rule owes its name to Vilfredo Pareto – an Italian economist who noticed that 80 per cent of Italy's income went to 20 per cent of the population. Business management thinker, Joseph M Juran, speculated that in business, and indeed many other aspects of life, 80 per cent of effects come from 20 per cent of causes.

If we look critically at what we do, day to day, we can see that, while not always exactly quantifiable (or *exactly* 80:20) many of our rewards in life come from a small amount of input, and often to increase these rewards we need to devote a disproportionate amount of time and effort to achieve more. We can also see in our work and business lives that in many cases the greatest amount of our income comes from the top 20 per cent of our clients and in a wage- or salary-based position 80 per cent of our productivity comes from 20 per cent of our time.

This situation certainly begs the question: "Why work five times more than I have to in order to earn 20 per cent more, or become 20 per cent more productive?"

Of course the answer is that Pareto's Law shows us that we get the majority of our results from the most effective 20 per cent of our time and energy, and to harness the power of this concept we must realise when to satisfice, and when to strive for even greater rewards, in spite of the disproportionate amount of time required to get there.

Pareto's Law and the art of satisficing are context

dependent.

In order to know when we are being effective in
reaching our goals and turning our dreams into reality, we must
be able to evaluate critically what we are putting time into and
ask ourselves a simple question: "Is it worth it?"

If the extra hours are going to take you to a cherished
goal, then of course it is worth it. If the hours are outweighed
by only a minimal increase or no increase in satisfaction, the
question is already redundant. What are you doing wasting your
time!

BE GENTLE WITH YOURSELF

A key tenet I believe of living as one of the time rich is to 'be
gentle with oneself'. When we are constantly striving to better
our position, past a point of a worthy return on our time
investment, we are doing anything but!

Chapter 6 Exercises

The BIG clear-out

This provides a great opportunity to clear out a whole lot of clutter and unnecessary items (and distraction) from your life. Travelling, a shift of living space or renovating are perfect times to reduce the amount of unnecessary 'things' you keep, but really there is never a bad time to do 'the big clear-out'.

This exercise is simple, but it does demand a fair bit of work. Nonetheless, the results are well worth the effort.

Begin by going through *everything* you own. You can start room by room, or in whatever way suits you best. There is no right or wrong simply the process that leads to less clutter and distraction.

For any item you have there are only three options:

1. Keep it
2. Sell it
3. Get rid of it

What to keep

Deciding what to keep is the hardest decision. We attach so much to things, even if they no longer serve us, and we worry about whether some situation will arise in which we might require an item – even if we haven't used it for a long time (or at all!).

There may come a time when you do need that particular set of hedge clippers, or there may be a time when you do get around to fixing up that old chair … or you may at some stage get back into fencing … but if you aren't doing it now, haven't done it for more than six months and if you haven't planned on doing it again soon, odds are you won't.

There are probably plenty of things you could conceivably use in the future, but simply holding on to things because there is some distant possibility of use is a waste of time, space and money.

For example, people find clothes hard to get rid of. But once they are gone it is pretty easy to forget them. If you haven't worn something for six months (except of course seasonal clothing such as winter jackets and thermals) then get rid of it. The amount of clothes we have is just ridiculous.

If you are staying in your house, use the following 'razor' for anything you are keeping:

'Will it live here?'

In other words, is that where you want the item?

If not – move it to its home! So often we leave things in places expecting to move them again later or waiting until we find a 'home' for them.

If you are moving to a new house or travelling, simply make a pile of all the things you are keeping.

What and how to sell

Also make a pile for things you are going to sell and things you are getting rid of.

You will be surprised that you can sell most things. Even if for only one dollar, it is still a better option to make a little money from discarded items and have them a) taken away by somebody else (always specify pick-up when selling, especially by online auction and selling sites – or have a yard sale), thereby reducing your costs, and b) have the item utilised by someone who has a need for it, rather than it becoming landfill.

I have made not inconsequential amounts of money when embarking on long-term travel by selling items I had no further use for – all of which helped me to be able to see and do even more.

What and how to trash

It is very tempting simply to put everything in a pile and take it to the tip; however, with the amount of things people accumulate over years of hoarding, they will have a huge number of things to throw out. In these times we need to make a concerted effort to dispose of our 'junk' as ethically as we can.

Wherever possible we should sell what we want to get rid of. It provides a little monetary 'wiggle room' for us, but also provides a new home and new usefulness for whatever we are getting rid of.

If we can't sell it, the next best option is to give it away for reuse or a new use.

Anything that can be recycled should be, and only when everything that can be sold, gifted, reused or recycled, has been disposed of should the rest be taken to the tip. Green material should of course be composted.

Reflections

An affirmation:

"I do my best, and my best is good enough." (Do you believe this?)

Do I accumulate the unnecessary?

Do I worry unduly about the future?

CHAPTER SEVEN

Creating Time

How to become a time magician

"EFFICIENCY IS INTELLIGENT LAZINESS."
~ DAVID DUNHAM

Do you feel that although you are only effective 20 per cent of the time, you need the other 80 per cent of the time to 'get into the swing of things'?

If this is the case, you may need to become *more effective*.

To get optimal return on our time, we need to stop being effective only between long periods of being ineffective. I define being 'ineffective' in this context as being idle or unproductive when you want to be productive. So, this still allows for those times we want to simply 'veg out' or play (which is crucial).

If we really want to live with an abundance of time, and a richness of time and experiences, and have more time and energy to do the things we love doing, and also to have more of the means to do it, we cannot afford to let 'dead time' become the window dressing to our productive time.

Creating 'time-blocks' for activities in your daily schedule is one of the easiest ways to become more effective with your time. Time-blocking is simply setting aside a certain period of time and deciding to do only one task within that time. Sounds simple, right?

Well, it is simple, but all too often we get distracted by the myriad tasks we have to complete, and we switch from one thing to another – dissipating our effectiveness and reducing our focus and productivity.

Procrastination and aversion also affect our ability to truly focus and 'get down to business'. When we don't want to do something (even if it's something we know we really *should* do) there are many ways we delay actually doing it.

Pushing 'send and receive' on our email program, checking our Myspace, Facebook and Twitter accounts and checking the headlines on Google news are just a few of the ways we delay the inevitable. The point is, though, that all these things, whilst possibly enjoyable, are not necessarily helping us *in the moment* to get the most out of our time.

Blocking out time is extremely simple. If you have to get a project done, simply set an amount of time and within that time focus solely on that task. Set your watch, or set a timer, and work away on the project until such time as you can do something else. You can also set a word limit, a 'must do' task or achievement, or any other *defined* and *quantifiable* measure for your 'block'. Then the only thing you need to do is sit down and actually do it.

I have found the most effective way for me to set aside time for writing is to simply prioritise it in my daily schedule and set a word count that I must achieve before I can turn my mind to other tasks. Even if the words I am putting on paper are not my best work (they can all be altered later) it at least provides the framework, and the 'critical mass' of information for my articles, books and lectures. My great friend and mentor Dr Ian Brooks gave me, when writing my first book, sage advice that I have carried with me since that day. He told me: "Finish your draft". He said many aspiring authors get hung up on writing, editing and rewriting *parts* of their book, without ever finishing a draft. In other words, they were honing the details without ever reaching the critical mass of information required to have a 'book'. This is true of any project and that's why giving it the time to simply make sure there is a solid base of work, information and material is crucial to success.

There are, of course, times when we are extremely motivated, inspired and creative, and it is at these times I write more and of a better quality too; however, if I only wrote during those times of energy and motivation, I would get no writing projects finished at all.

'Boundless energy is not a requirement for achieving your goals, but boundless perseverance is!'

~ *From* Choosing You!

Do the Single Most Important Thing in Your Day First!

Whenever I have been at my most productive, and more importantly at my most *effective*, I have applied this rule in some form.

We often get 'bogged down' by the inevitably long list of things that becomes attracted to our to-do lists, and the cycle of slowly working our way through them can be confusing and at times even a little soul-destroying! In reality, though, much of what is on our to-do list is not so much important, as necessary. In other words, many of the tasks we have to do are simply related to compliance or have been left so long as to become urgent; however, they are not necessarily the things a) we either have a passion for doing, or b) that will help put us where we want to be in life.

For many of these tasks I would highly recommend a cut-throat application of the four Ds outlined later in this chapter (especially the dumping and delegating portions), and for the rest I suggest choosing just one (or at most four, with less than three being preferable) task that is critical in any given day. It should be the things that if you did them only (and nothing else at all) you would feel happy with your day.

Many people have written about similar themes, and I have found from experience, because I like to have a single focus (as it keeps my somewhat scattered and ethereal nature in check … and because it allows me the potential to get to the beach a little earlier!), that simply having one mission-critical task in any given day works extraordinarily well. It might be, for me, that I write a certain number of words on my current book, blog post or magazine article, or that I spend a certain amount of time on a research project. Of course it is very seldom the only thing I do in a given day, but it *is* what I deem to be the most important, and by setting it up as such, I must make sure it is completed and given its due importance in my mind's eye and in my schedule.

The laser-like focus that the *'one thing today'* rule allows is to reduce the potential for us to get stuck doing low return, and often draining activities, such as checking email (possibly the worst thing you can do first thing in the day) or Facebook, or finding ourselves in the awful position of having wasted a day doing non-time-critical chores at the expense of doing the things we are passionate about.

Often doing the important things presents a block for us because if we actually start to work on projects we hold dear to our very core being, we become committed to them. This is a very challenging position, because when we begin to work towards our dreams, we open ourselves up to criticism. We fear that if we create something it will not be seen as good enough by others, and we fear we won't be able to make money from our efforts in creative or expression-based fields and we fear the loss of feelings of security if we begin to stray from the norm. All these fears are valid but if we do not put time and effort into the things that matter to us, we instead put time and effort into things that are inconsequential. This is a complete waste of our most precious resource. It matters not what the artist does, except for doing her art. It matters not what others think of the 'art' or the 'work' because she can only do that for which she craves.

ALLOCATE TIME TO THE MOST IMPORTANT …
NOT JUST THE URGENT.

It is crucial to set time aside for the important things that we most want to be doing with our days and prioritise these. But of course, it is also crucial to actually get done some of the compliance-based activities in our days. The way we can deal with this is outlined below in the four Ds of time effectiveness; however, one thing that distracts us is communication. This used to involve mainly email communication but now also includes all the various social media.

I *love* social media. I think social networking is super-cool, and it gives me a great way to stay connected to my clients, friends and readers all over the world at the touch of a button. But it can also be used as a tool for distraction and procrastination. What is an amazing conduit for connection can easily become a replacement for real human interaction and a distraction from what is really most important for us to be doing?

Setting aside time for communications is a great way to deal with this. Simply setting aside a time (I have used 11 am and 3 pm, for example) as times to clear emails (and make sure you do actually 'clear' emails and other online communication, not just peruse it), check Facebook and Twitter, and post to Tumblr and my blog. When doing this I am more focused on replying to people (a good thing), connecting, and I still allow myself to 'play' for a time as well. It's the best of both worlds.

Make Tasks Disappear

There is a way to reduce mental stress and anguish and become more time effective in the process, and that is to make tasks disappear.

There are some simple tricks you can use to become a time magician.

Any task that comes to you can be dealt with using the four 'Ds' of time effectiveness (adapted loosely from *Getting Things Done* by David Allen).

Dump it
Do It
Delegate It
Defer It

Dump It

Why would you let something hang around in your mailbox, inbox or task list if it didn't actually 'need' to be done?

Having already evaluated some of the low gain activities and low reward 'things' to cut from our lives, this is another way to free up time. Try this: If something unimportant pops into your inbox just delete it. Don't worry about whether it might be important in ten months' time or that you might read it for interest 'when you get the time' – because you won't. Just delete it and be done with it.

I used to sign up for all sorts of health and wellness journals, newsletters and ezines. I figured I had to stay up to date. The reality, however, is that I never got around to reading them! They sat in my inbox and ended up stressing me out because I felt at some stage, I had to read them. Their mere presence put them into my mental to-do list, which for most of us has a tendency to be too long already.

It then dawned on me that I was working with clients, day in and day out, solving their problems and writing articles and books, and giving lectures, all of which required me to stay up to date by reading magazines, journals and studies in relation to what I was doing. So, I was already doing a lot of research; however, the difference was that all the research I was doing was solving problems or producing material. The end result was the same, because no two clients are the same, and no two projects I become involved with are identical, so I was still acquiring a wide breadth of knowledge. In other words, it was an effective use of my time. And to be honest, I do a fair bit of 'playing' in libraries, bookstores and on the net reading all sorts of things that help me to expand my knowledge and my practice, but I do it for fun and either a) when I have time that I have put aside for it, or b) when I simply need a break, and it's a welcome distraction. Feeling compelled to read all the e-information coming into my inbox certainly wasn't.

And so, I unsubscribed from *everything*. If I need information it is easy to find nowadays, and the time I save not opening and inevitably deleting those emails is time I have given back to myself.

Do It

Do the important things now.

When unfulfilled, tasks – particularly those from which there is no escape, no matter how far into cyberspace we run from them – are a mental burden sitting in the back of our mind adding to our overall stress load until they are dealt with. So, no matter how hard we try to avoid the inevitable there comes a time when we simply have to do it.

This is particularly true when the activities only take a matter of minutes. The mental burden of remembering yet another thing to do outweighs the minimal time it takes to actually do it. So, when these low time input activities come up, it is far better to simply do them, then and there, rather than having them weigh on your mind.

A simple rule is that if a task comes across your desk (or cyberdesk) that will take less than five minutes to complete, do it.

Remember you will only receive communications during times you have set aside for them, so doing these simple, immediate tasks will not distract you from more important things, but if you leave them for later the mental burden of several tasks you need to keep track of will be distracting.

Delegate It

Why would you do something if someone else could do it more effectively or at less financial or time cost?

Learning to delegate tasks is one of the keys to success for freeing up your time. And in the modern age of new media and new commerce, many options to delegate are at little or no cost.

I first started in business when I was still at college. I opened a nutritional supplement store with a friend. The business grew extremely quickly, and we soon expanded into mail order and online sales. This was a great source of additional revenue for us, but at the time it was still a fairly labour-intensive operation.

Orders would come by phone or via an online notification. Our staff would then charge the customer's credit card by calling the bank to manually approve the transaction. The order would then be packaged, and the courier called for a pick-up.

While this process may not seem difficult, it was somewhat unnecessary, time-consuming and provided just one more thing that needed to be done (which always provides that little extra mental).

We were not as efficient as we could have been, partly because we didn't know any better and partly because point of sale technology was not as advanced then. Over time we began trying to expedite our processes. We began by implementing easier point of sale credit card processing, third-party 'real time' credit card verification, and later; fully automated 'pick and pack' sales and logistics services. Eventually I no longer had physical locations, but instead an automated sales system that put money in my bank every month with little or no direct contact work from me – and without the need for staff.

In publishing the process has become even more efficient, and through a combination of print on demand publishing and logistics, e-media sales, third-party retail sales and commission-only agents, I can focus on the important task of doing what I love doing – writing about the things I love. Not selling, packaging and delivering products.

Knowing what to delegate, and to whom, and what to focus my efforts on has not only increased the available time for 'me' but also reduced my costs and made my businesses more efficient, all at less risk to me.

Win … win … win.

Delegating effectively, and with little cost is becoming easier and easier in our e-driven world. There are countless reputable outsourcing and 'virtual assistant' companies, especially in emerging economies like India and the Philippines. It is becoming increasingly easy to deal with companies in a purely 'remote' fashion and have single or ongoing tasks completed by offshore and local specialists for a fraction of what it once cost.

Websites like e-lance (www.elance.com) and others make it easy to have freelance professionals bid for projects for which you previously may have had little option but to pay top dollar for. Online solutions in accounting, logistics, publishing and marketing are providing low- and, in many cases, no-cost options.

Outside of increased cashflow and time, an often-underestimated benefit of delegating is that you simply don't have to do things you don't want to do.

If you can't stand doing accounts, then I would suggest you don't do them. Any task that provides mental stress and anguish that you can realistically afford to have done by someone else, you can and perhaps should delegate. If you can't afford it, you have two options:

- Find a way to be able to afford it.
- Find a viable, lower cost solution.

In the modern economy there may be ways you can

simplify other areas of your life or business so you are able to delegate the tasks you don't enjoy. This can often provide additional stress-reducing benefits of simplification.

There are plenty of low- and no-cost options in many areas now. Some of these will be evaluated in the chapter Become a Freek!

Defer It

Having tasks sitting around without any sort of end date, conclusion or plan plays on your mind, and while it may not always be taking your time directly, it certainly can provide residual stress and anxiety that can affect the quality and enjoyment of your time. But as soon as there is some type of resolution to the problem – even if the task is not finished – much of the anxiety is put to rest. Simply having set aside a time to do the task takes away the thoughts of 'when am I going to do this?'.

By writing it down and making it time-accountable we remove it from our mental to-do list. This has a profound effect and is why writing things down, having a schedule, and making lists of things to do is so important – it removes the obligation to remember everything.

Deferring tasks does not mean just putting them to one side. When we defer a task, if we simply put it on the back burner, it still hangs around as mental rubbish tapping our energy. When we defer a task or activity, we must make it time accountable. This brings us back to time-blocking. When we are unable to either dump, delegate or do a task, we must find a time when we could do it, then diarise that time for the task. That way it is dealt with and no longer remains something we have to worry about – until it becomes a 'do' task. Until that time, at least, mentally we can let it go.

For more information on Time Effectiveness I highly recommend: *Getting Things Done: The Art of Stress-Free Productivity* by David Allen.

CUT LOW-GAIN ACTIVITIES

Some things we do in our daily lives are simply a waste of time.

These 'low-gain' activities are usually time-fillers. Examples include watching TV, searching the net and other relatively passive experiences. Now, I'm not for a second saying we should avoid TV and the Internet, but if we want to maximise our enjoyment of our time, to pursue goals and dreams, the decisions to do these things should be *powerful*. We should be watching TV for the enjoyment the show provides, and we should search the net for things of interest. In other words, we should spend our time wisely in pursuit of things we want – not merely waste time because we don't know what to do or because we are waiting for something else to happen.

When you are bored and wondering what to do, instead of thinking of what you could be doing, think of what you would most like to be doing. If it is watching a great TV show then go and watch that show; if it's to do some research online, by all means go and do that, but I'm sure that when we actually change our mindset to filling our available time with things that give us joyous experiences, instead of simply looking for something to do, our chances for time-wasting are much reduced.

I have, for example, gone for long periods without owning or watching a television. And I haven't missed channel surfing in the hopes of finding a show that I find vaguely amusing or distracting. I have too many other things to do that really excite me! However, if there are shows I enjoy, I prefer to watch them on DVD or online so I can watch at my leisure, at a time that suits me and without advertising interruptions. It also means I don't need to own a TV, as I can watch it on my laptop. If you really enjoy watching a big screen TV, this last point will not apply to you, but, for me at least, having a TV is just one more aspect of the 'norm' that I can do without, thereby adding more simplicity to my life and reducing my relative cost burden.

Don't 'Work' if There is Nothing to Do!

This concept also seems simple – right?

I can almost hear you saying, "Why would I work when there's nothing to do? I don't do that …"

But don't be so sure. Have there ever been times when you have sat at your computer, staring at the screen, trying to get some energy or inspiration from somewhere, or clicking 'send and receive' on your email programme, waiting for the crucial last piece of information needed for you to complete a project?

During these episodes you are spending time, but you're not really working, and you're certainly not having fun – so you are wasting time. If you're not able to be productive you are better off doing something else or simply taking time to relax and chill out.

Don't 'Work' if You Are Not Being Productive

Sometimes there are plenty of things to do. You have a to-do list as long as your arm and you know that you should be working. But you are tired, unmotivated or you just can't get a clear idea of a way forward with a particular task.

Commitment to a task, work ethic and getting 'stuck in' are all imperative for accomplishing things, but we also need to be pragmatic. If you are not making headway on a task you might, in many instances, be better off taking a break.

If I find myself with writer's block, or not being productive for more than a few minutes, I stop and take a break. Often if I'm tired from training or not getting enough sleep – salsa dancing till the early hours of the morning can take its toll – I'll do one of my favourite things: siesta. Or I'll go for a walk, meditate, go to the gym or even better, take myself out on a solo date where I do something I have wanted to do – like go to the local art gallery or to a movie. Even a small break when you are feeling like everything is getting on top of you can be enough to kick-start your creative fire and give you the energy you need to launch yourself back into your day with gusto.

Stop 'Getting Through'

It is a symptom of our modern lifestyle, and our addiction to rushing, movement and activity, that we hold a constant desire to 'get through' tasks that we are involved in. When we seek to simply 'get through' tasks though, we become overly focused on an indeterminate future that we think will be more agreeable than the present. This can lead to us living for a future fantasy what will be, without ever really appreciating the present moment. On a physiological level it also encourages us to ignore the subtle signals from our body telling us what we need and therefore what we should be doing.

I see this when dealing with patients in my naturopathic practice. A common scenario in people's working days is that they will be involved in a task and they begin to get hungry, but instead of eating, they think 'Oh, I'll just get through this and then I'll have something to eat.'

The problem with doing this is that as soon as they say, 'I'll just get through this' and subvert their natural instinct to eat, they are telling their bodies 'I *need* to get this done', and on a subconscious and physiological level it becomes a *survival imperative*. When faced with a task necessary for survival, our bodies will produce stimulatory hormones (norepinephrine, epinephrine and dopamine) to allow us to remain alert and active and to encourage continued physical performance and mental acuity. They also act as appetite suppressants. Have you ever noticed that when you continue to work in spite of being hungry, you stop being hungry? Well that's the reason why.

This can continue for some time, and I'm sure you would all have noticed that when you get into this state you can work for hours on end and simply 'forget' to eat. But when you get a chance to relax what happens?

You crave everything under the sun!

You have been through a period of deprivation and your body, once the perceived 'threat' is gone, seeks to replenish itself by elevating blood glucose rapidly, by eating sugar or highly processed carbohydrates and consuming the most calories possible, from fat, being the highest caloric macronutrient.

This is what many people experience when they get home after work, having not eaten well during the day; and this is the reason there was a line-up for doughnuts at the Tim

Horton's located under my Vancouver office at around three o'clock every day.

When we tell our bodies just to 'get through', it responds as if we are in danger. I mean, really, why on earth would we *not* eat food when we are hungry? Surely, we must a) be out of food and need to go out hunting and gathering or b) be about to be attacked by a sabre-toothed tiger. We can see then why this response is so valuable. You don't want to be eaten by a sabre-toothed tiger, now do you? However, in the modern world we tend towards overusing this 'fight or flight' response and as a result are overstressed. Acute stress is something the body can deal with well –running away from a predator, chasing down game etc. – and is actually a necessary and healthy part of life, but it needs to be in small doses and for tasks that can be completed then put aside and alternated with periods of rest.

Chronic stress is when we are constantly utilising this stress response, and this is what we tend to do in the modern world – we beat ourselves up with too many perceived survival imperatives without listening to the signals our body is giving us. I see this exemplified particularly in two other major habits that people have nowadays: caffeine and snacks.

Caffeine

I want to say firmly that I am not against coffee. In fact, I love the stuff, but because I do, I need to make sure I do not overuse it. And unfortunately, overuse it, we do.

Caffeine is the world's most used drug. In fact, the total world consumption of caffeine equates to 70 mg (approx. two cups of tea or a shot and a half of Arabica espresso) per day for every man, woman and child on the planet[6]. In North America up to 90 per cent of the population ingest caffeine daily at an average of 200 mg–280 mg. This to me is chronic use. Coffee can give performance benefits, and it has many healthful properties – providing certain beneficial alkaline compounds and antioxidants, to name two – but it also provides the stimulatory response that we all tend to over utilise. The reality is that most North Americans are tired and exhausted, and we subvert what we need to be doing by taking stimulants to just get us through our days.

If we are tired should we:

a)   Have a nap (or even better re-evaluate our sleep routine, diet and lifestyle habits so we are more rested and have better energy reserve)?

b)   Gulp down an enormous coffee?

The answer by now should be obvious.

---

[6] Prog Clin Biol Res. 1984;158:185-213.
Caffeine consumption.
Gilbert RM

Snacks

Snacking is good – right?

I'm not so sure. I am a fan of eating frequent meals but too often snacks are seen simply as a means by which we get through until our next proper meal.

When this happens, we tend to overeat at the larger meals and under-eat at snack time. This serves to create big rises and falls in blood glucose, causing poor energy and potential for fat gain, but also rises and falls in blood protein levels, which negatively affect protein synthesis and thus muscle retention, metabolic rate and repair from training. Not to mention the fact that many snack foods are nutritionally devoid.

Snacking also promotes 'eating on the run', something I discourage my clients from doing. It is much better from a digestive standpoint to stop, sit down and eat a meal, which encourages more effective peristalsis and motility as well as gastric and digestive enzyme efficacy, and it really doesn't take a lot of time to do this. In fact, I have measured time and efficiency of stopping and being total and present in the act of eating v. eating in front of the computer and trying to multitask by doing emails or other things. It is actually more time effective to do one thing well than trying to do many things at once, as our effectiveness at doing those tasks is reduced past a point of diminishing returns.

By eating frequent, balanced, quality meals, as compared to a few big meals separated by snacks, we help to break the cycle of 'getting through', and we provide more consistent nutrition and 'nutrient density' to help us perform – and look! – better.

So, in essence we need to stop 'getting through' and start listening to our bodies, as they will tell us most if not all we need to know. We are not the 'ghost in the machine' that simply drives a biochemical vehicle, so we can't continue driving our bodies into the ground through stress and overwork. Our physiology is not expendable, as it is an integral part of our mind-body-spirit complex. It is a vibrant collection of interdependent cells with independent and collective consciousness, and by honouring this wonderful community we honour ourselves, and we reap the rewards in a greater richness and quality of our most precious resource – time.

'When you're hungry – eat; when you're tired – sleep.'
~ Buddhist Proverb

GIVING YOURSELF THE GIFT OF TIME

The 'Self Date'

This is a concept I picked up from *The Artist's Way* by Julia Cameron. She advocates, as part of the process outlined in the book, that on at least one day of the week you should plan to do something for yourself, by yourself.

The important thing is that it should be something you really want to do. Use it as a chance to have experiences. That after all is the goal of maximising your time and the goal of this book – to be spending your 'time account' on experiences that enrich and fulfil your life.

Often, we do end up *not* doing certain things that we really want to do because we don't have someone to do them with. Conversely, we end up spending a lot of our time alone simply doing the same things we have always done – sitting on the couch watching TV. The amount of great films I missed over the years by not having someone to go with when I had time to go. Well never again.

Time Wasters and Time Wasting

You wouldn't throw money away, would you?

Then why are we so happy to throw away so much of our valuable time?

There are so many times in life when we end up 'filling in time' with things that we neither enjoy nor get any real return out of. Phrases like 'killing time' and 'filling in time', show our attitude to time. When we say these things, we are living in a future-focused mindset that stops us from living in the now – the only time that we can ever actually live in. It may be we are waiting to go out somewhere, waiting for a call from a special person or waiting for an opportunity we know is just around the corner, but if those things are going to happen then they will, in good time. If there are things you can do now to hasten their arrival, then shouldn't you be doing that instead of killing time? And if there isn't anything you can do, then killing time is simply wasting time, and you could be doing something else wonderful, whilst knowing that more wondrous experiences are on their way.

This is not to say that we need to be constantly 'doing something'. In fact, some of my favourite times are when I am doing very little. The difference is that if I have chosen to do nothing then that is a powerful thing. I may need to recharge, to think, go for a walk, meditate or simply lie on the couch with some convenience food and watch a DVD. Intention is what matters. 'Killing time' is a resignation. Doing 'nothing' because you want and need it – in reality, just being idle so you can recharge – is a powerful choice.

Don't resign yourself to idle time; make a powerful choice to make it great.

Killing time is suicide.

Making powerful choices allows us to live our lives on purpose. Any time you find yourself thinking, 'I need to kill some time'

STOP …

and DON'T!

There are so many occasions, when we have finished 'killing time', and we think, 'Oh, I wish I had done *that* instead.'

As we have already investigated, knowing the things we want to do, and experience is a result of looking at who we are now and dreaming the person we want to become. Without having taken the time to evaluate and analyse these things we cannot know what we should be doing in those precious moments when we need not be doing the urgent. It is at these times we end up doing what is ultimately more important for the person we are and want to be. Moments of completely free will and opportunity are beautiful, precious gifts that we give ourselves. And if you haven't looked at your life and decided what you want to be doing and achieving, those free moments are the perfect opportunity to do it.

I love nothing more than getting to the end of a task, having some time to stop, reflect and chill out, and take my notebook down to the beach, walk around the park, sit in the sand and reconnect with life.

'Leisure is not the privilege of those who have the time, but the virtue of those who take the time.'

~ Brother David Steindl-Rast

Planning your day

Once you are into your day it is already too late to plan it.

By the time you sit down at your computer you will automatically begin to do the most urgent tasks and non-urgent communication simply because you are in a reactive mode of operating, and this may not be the most effective way to work to achieve your goals *and* to achieve your most fulfilling day.

Plan your day the day before

At the end of your working day take a few moments to plan your next day.

- Choose one to three time-critical tasks that you will definitely complete the following day. These are your must-dos – everything else is a bonus. Use the rationale that if you only get these particular tasks done you will be completely satisfied with your working day.

- Block-time these tasks and prioritise them, that is, *do them first.*

- Then block out time to do other non-essential but important things – like communication (email, social networking, IM etc.). Again 'block' times for this so you are doing it effectively and not wasting time checking, rechecking and generally drifting in cyberspace.

Schedule one 'self-date' for your week

Each and every week I want you to schedule at least one 'date' with yourself, and by yourself, to do something you have either really wanted to do or that you *love* doing.

Set aside at least three hours for this date and make sure you schedule the time for it. If others make demands of you during this time simply say, "Sorry, I have an appointment." Remember that we need to honour ourselves by making and keeping 'self-appointments' as much as we honour others by making and keeping appointments with them. You are worth it.

If you have a partner, it is a great idea to set a date with them too. This is *in addition* to your self-date though, not *instead* of it.

In years of practice I have found this simple practice of being with your partner, spending quality time and actually *doing* something, compared to just being around them, can transform a relationship and provide much-needed vibrancy back into the interpersonal dynamic.

Reflections

Do I fill my time with distractions?

Do these distractions improve my life or simply fill time?

Do I set aside time for myself and the things I love?

Do I set aside time for others?

Could I honour myself more by giving ME the gift of time?

Golden Moments

How to realise the value of a moment

"YOU MUST LIVE IN THE PRESENT, LAUNCH YOURSELF ON EVERY WAVE, FIND YOUR ETERNITY IN EACH MOMENT."
~ HENRY DAVID THOREAU

There is only one time in life that we can live and that is in the moment.

To many this seems a moot point, as they equate being *alive* with really *living*. It's easy to believe we are living in the moment because it is the only time that we can live; however, if we are constantly thinking about the future, attached to outcomes or worrying about the past and having those dreaded 'past attacks', we are not really 'living' but are merely 'alive', which is our default position. And for our happiness and satisfaction, and to truly be in line with our life's purpose, it is not enough. We need to reconnect with the moment.

MINDFULNESS AND MATERIALISM

Mindfulness is seeing things for what they are. It is being open to what is going on around you, without attachment and without 'reaction', moment to breaking moment. It is developing the 'watcher' or the 'observer' within.

Our minds are perpetual motion machines that create thought after thought. Mindfulness is recognising that these thoughts are transient – they are not *us*.

By observing our thoughts and emotions, and by developing the watcher within, we can see that our thoughts are not us. There is something deeper than that. We know this simply because we can become mindful, we can 'watch' our thoughts and emotions arise, so we know they are things that happen and are in fact things that we 'do', so they cannot therefore be 'us'.

Developing mindfulness is essential to maximise our enjoyment and appreciation of time. If we are not fully in each breaking moment, how can we hope to enjoy it?

It is also essential for realising what is important for our deepest happiness and, on the other hand, what we are doing or trying to possess merely to boost our ego.

From Choosing You!
Developing mindfulness can be very basic. Meditation has been used for centuries to develop mindfulness. Many eastern (and also western) religions

and many schools of philosophy and psychology include mindfulness in some form as either a fundamental goal or tenet.

There are several ways you can encourage mindfulness in your life. I strongly recommend you put some time (as little as 10 minutes) each and every day into one mindfulness activity. You can do the same activity every day at the same time, at different times or perform different activities as you feel like it. An activity that suits one person will not suit another. Be a power unto yourself. The main thing is that you do it.

MEDITATION AND MINDFULNESS

With meditation and the development of mindfulness we are more likely to be living in the present moment. We are also more likely to see when we are acting in ways that are not in our highest good and not leading to the life we want to live.

Becoming more mindful is one of the key ways we begin to release ego attachments and, therefore, also begin to attach less to extrinsic reward and become more aware of what makes us happier in a true sense, not that of transient ecstasy.

I have a long history of meditation. I personally love mindfulness of breath and have practised this form of meditation in its various forms as part of a Vipassana practice I have been involved with since I was a child. The breath is timeless, it is always there, a valuable tool to help encourage mindfulness.

I used to meditate every day in this fashion for at least 20 minutes, almost always first thing in the morning. Over the years, though, I noticed that my meditation and life began to become integrated (or I like to say 'wonderfully confused'), and I began to 'meditate' less frequently and was less rigid about the time and style of my meditation; however, my life has continued to become more and more 'mindful' over time.

Years later, I now have the pleasure of meditating and praying with many spiritual teachers and groups around the world, in many different ways, and I have been able to integrate aspects of these teachings into my own practice and my pastoral and spiritual coaching work.

There are many other forms of meditation that encourage mindfulness, and I encourage you simply to find what works for you and what you connect most with. The goal is in the doing and in finding a conduit for greater connection to *life* which will often be framed as a direct connection to source or the divine. The frames we wrap around it are inconsequential, and the means by which we connect are simply the 'finger pointing to the moon'. Don't get hung up on the finger or you'll miss that glimpse of the moon!

By becoming more mindful and more aware, we can begin to see the life we would like to be living and the person we would like to be. Once we have noticed this, we can then begin to create the actions and behaviours that will lead us towards it.

Affirmations & Belief Statements

Positive affirmations or 'belief statements' are one of the most powerful ways we can begin to engender the subconscious thought processes that allow us to live the lives we want to be living.

So much of what we do is determined by our subconscious mind and is under the level of our conscious awareness. This subconscious activity allows us to breathe, to have a semi-autonomous heartbeat and to provide for all the myriad cellular functions that occur moment to moment in life. The subconscious or autonomic mind is therefore a crucial survival tool, as we would not want to forget to 'beat our hearts' or breathe. But the autonomic/subconscious mind is completely *arational* – in other words, rationality does not play any role in what the subconscious mind projects and, in turn, what we act upon.

The subconscious mind is the level where our beliefs and our conditioned behaviours reside. These beliefs and behaviours become patterned over time and become ingrained as patterns of action that we live out, often without realising. And although many of these are useful and help to protect us from danger and to react to stimuli appropriately, so that we survive calamity, we may also pattern self-limiting and negative beliefs, which lead to self-limiting behaviours and actions. These reactions to stimuli may have served a survival purpose in the past, but this need might not be required anymore;

however, the patterning and its effect on our actions remains. The reactions we develop may not have served any survival need either, but the same survival mechanisms kicked in to create certain patterns of action.

I can illustrate this point with an example from my clinical mind–body practice.

I was treating a young woman with severe food allergies, – particularly all manner of dairy and wheat. She was from a large Italian family, and upon investigating her family history, it became clear that mealtimes, which inevitably involved a lot of pasta, cheese and bread, were extraordinarily stressful times. She explained that at mealtimes there were often heated discussions, arguments and tension, that although considered 'normal' for her family, and not violent or abusive, were to her a very stressful time. As a retiring, somewhat shy person her stress response would go into overdrive when she sat down to dinner.

She related how even just knowing mealtime was approaching would initiate the tell-tale signs of an adrenal stress response – increased heart rate, sweaty palms, flushing.

Now because the subconscious is not rational and because it is simply a survival mechanism, it equates stimuli and response. When a particular stimulus or set of stimuli is present and there is a stress response, over time those stimuli will initiate a stress response or negative reaction regardless of whether it is consciously or rationally justified.

So, it makes complete sense that being repeatedly exposed to the sights, smells and chemical constituents of certain foods, in the presence of a highly charged, stress-filled environment, would ingrain lifelong negative reactions to those foods. This type of reaction has also been noted when looking at comorbidities of panic disorder: a condition characterised by severe, acute episodes of anxiety that can be quite debilitating. These severe, stress-filled episodes have been noted to increase allergic reaction[7].

Note: With the use of belief repatterning and clinical hypnotherapy, this client was able to release her allergies and sensitivities to these food groups and is now able to eat dairy and wheat – although she is still justifiably cautious – without ill effects.

This case is a good real-world example of many of the breakthroughs in the area of medical science known as *psychoneuroimmunology* (PNI).

Psychoneuroimmunology is the study of how psychological factors affect immune function and has shown repeatedly that immunity, of which allergies are a function, can be affected and dictated by psychological factors and behavioural conditioning.

---

[7] Br J Clin Psychol. 1997 Feb;36 (Pt 1):51-62.
The psychoimmunological association of panic disorder and allergic reaction

A 2008 study published in psychotherapy and psychosomatics exposed patients to a 'novel-tasting drink' followed by a histamine receptor antagonist, to reduce symptoms of allergic rhinitis, for five days, followed by a nine-day drug 'washout'. Patients were then exposed to either the novel- tasting drink followed by a placebo, water followed by placebo, or water followed by the drug (desloratadine).

The patients taking the water followed by placebo still had a reduction in self-reported symptoms and had a lower response to skin prick testing. The group who took the novel-tasting drink solution followed by placebo had a similar response to the drug group for self- reported symptoms, skin prick test and *for decreased basophil activation*[8].

This and other studies show not only the value of the mind–body link in being able to reduce disease and disorder in the body, but also the ability of the body to actively condition itself to new patterns of behaviour and new reactions to stimuli that are more conducive to the person we want to be and the life we want to be living.

Negative and self-limiting beliefs have been patterned over time. It is difficult to 'un-train' these patterns because they are beneath the control of the conscious mind, but we can, over time, repattern negative behaviours, and like any other learning it takes effort, concentration and repetition. Using

[8] Psychother Psychosom. 2008;77(4):227-34. Epub 2008 Apr 16.
Behavioral conditioning of antihistamine effects in patients with allergic rhinitis. Goebel MU, Meykadeh N, Kou W, Schedlowski M, Hengge UR.

positive affirmations and belief statements is a great way to do this.

Present tense, personal and positive

The subconscious mind operates solely in the 'now', so for belief repatterning to be effective, affirmation and belief statements must be made in the present tense. The idea of saying, for example, that 'I will be a champion' is somewhat nonsensical for the subconscious mind as there is no context for what 'will be', only for what *is*.

There is also less neurological effect from attempting to visualise or imagine what will be. In a nutshell, the brain's internal circuitry is activated in exactly the same way when we imagine doing something as if we are actually doing it. And of course, thinking of doing it is putting us in the present moment of doing it.

The huge power of this present tense application of belief statements is much older than the present New Age implications so often attached to it, such as the Law of Attraction etc. For example, it is even mentioned in the Bible as one of the fundamental aspects of prayer. In the gospel of St Mark, Jesus says: "All things for which you pray and ask, believe that you have received them, and they shall be granted to you."[9] And perhaps prayer, when relieved of its religious trappings, is simply the application of powerful affirmations and belief statements.

---

[9] Mark 11:24 New American Standard Bible

Belief statements and affirmations must also be personal. 'I' is one of the most powerful words one can use in creating belief statements. For you to begin to believe you *must* be talking to yourself in the first person.

If we are trying to engender positive actions and positive changes to our lives, the messages we provide to ourselves must also be positive. This much seems obvious, but I have seen countless times in practice that in spite of ourselves we often seek a positive outcome by framing our self statements in the negative. This is particularly true when we are trying to 'not' to do something – like smoking or overeating – because not doing it is best for our highest good. If someone wants to get in better physical shape, for example, they could say to themselves, "I don't want to be fat," or they could frame it as, "I want to be lean and muscular." Say these statements now. As you say them silently to yourself what images are projected?

When we frame things in words, we must be very aware of what we are creating on a subconscious level.

Try the following exercise, but first I want to you *not* to think of a pink elephant. Whatever you do, DO NOT think of an elephant.

See what happened! You *cannot* stop yourself from thinking about something when it is mentioned, so to programme new, positive beliefs effectively we must think only of the positive aspects of what we want to do. To use the previous example of getting in better physical shape, the desire not to be overweight is most effectively achieved by encouraging the visualisation and affirmation of being lean and muscular now, and this is most effectively created as a belief statement by removing 'I want to be' and replacing with 'I am'. Even though we know that consciously this is not true now, our subconscious does not have that luxury, and if we imagine and tell ourselves that it *is* true *now*, we will allow it to be so in the future. By extension if we have told ourselves that something *is not* true then on an insidious level, we will self-sabotage so that it will never become true.

This is a concept foreign to many. We tend to hold a very puritanical work view, that if we put in place the steps towards achieving something, and then do the work involved with that process, inevitably we will achieve what we have worked towards. However, when we consider that the subconscious is a finely-honed survival machine, and if we have told it over and over again that we can't achieve something, it will equate that achievement with danger. In other words, it will 'think' that achieving the goal will result in harm and will resist achievement of that goal. It will therefore place blocks in our path that will prevent us from doing what we consciously want to do.

These blocks could be as simple as affecting our perception of the world around us so that we don't notice things and people in our immediate physical and social environment who could be conducive to the achieving of a goal. Or it could bring to conscious attention things around us that are counterproductive to the achievement of our goal. After all, we do only bring to our *conscious* attention a very small fraction of what we actually see, hear and smell around us. And what we do bring to conscious attention is what is considered by us subconsciously to be the most crucial for our survival. If noticing something is seen as detrimental to our survival, it makes sense that we won't notice it.

On the other hand, where situations, people and environments are considered by the subconscious to serve a need for us, we will notice in our environment things that will help to make that service a reality. And so, we can, sometimes, attract negative people and relationships detrimental to our highest good into our lives. There is tantalising evidence that we may even develop illness, injury and pain in order to prevent ourselves from achieving certain things. As I have stated this is *out of our conscious control,* so it is not a function of laziness or lack of work ethic or desire but is simply how we have conditioned ourselves.

We can pattern ourselves into positive action instead of remaining a victim of our conditioning.

VISUALISATIONS

Visualisation, like affirmations and belief statements, are a powerful way to begin to retrain our subconscious minds and to influence real neurophysiological change, to encourage us to be where we want to be, as the person we want to be, achieving the things we want to achieve.

They should, like belief statements, be an encapsulation of what you want to be true, but this time in a visual context. Therefore, we should be imagining situations that we want to become true, as if they are true now, and with as much detail as possible.

I have noticed through my work with elite athletes that many of the top performers do this instinctively – top weightlifters, for example, may visualise themselves on the platform performing a lift effortlessly and with perfect technique. By doing this they actually fire the exact same neural pathways as if they were performing the lift. Several studies have shown that strength can be improved up to two-thirds as effectively through the use of visualisation as actually performing an exercise[10], and that fine and gross motor skills, such as shooting a basketball free throw, can be drastically improved through visualization[11].

A common image projection is also to imagine oneself having already won. The image of standing on the dais receiving your medal is a powerful one. In contrast negative

---

[10] Neuropsychologia. 2004;42(7):944-56. Links
From mental power to muscle power--gaining strength by using the mind.
Ranganathan VK, Siemionow V, Liu JZ, Sahgal V, Yue GH

[11] Percept Mot Skills. 1992 Dec;75(3 Pt 2):1243-53
Kearns DW, Crossman J.
Effects of a cognitive intervention package on the free-throw performance of
varsity basketball players during practice and competition

patterns of self-worth can create belief patterns of not being *able* to win; even rationally there seems no good reason why this should be true.

CREATING SPECIFIC LIFE ACTIONS

By knowing what we want and then creating the intention for it to happen, we set the base for being *able* to achieve what we want out of life. If we don't have the self-belief that we can achieve, we will not be able to. But once we do have it, the achievement of our goals and the reaching of our dreams is dependent upon action.

I reiterate that 'talk is cheap, and dreams are free … we are defined by our actions'.

If we have a particular goal and ambition, there will be activities and exercises we need to do in order to attain it.

Actions include things like starting an exercise and nutrition routine if, for example, your goal is to lose weight. Once the belief pattern has been established in the positive, the action plan must match the goal, and the actions that will get you to your goal must be done consistently.

The Importance of Daily Reflection

I wrote of the importance of reflection in *Choosing You!* We can – when we have a better conscious appreciation of the type of person we want to be and the life we want to be living, and when we have developed greater mindfulness and awareness – begin to change our daily patterns of action.

In spite of our best efforts, though, there will be times when we slip into old habits of action, and when these are negative, they may derail our efforts for self-improvement. Often because conditioned behaviours are so heavily ingrained, we may not even realise that we have acted in ways, throughout our day, that are leading us away from our dreams. Reflections can be valuable in these situations.

I have found that even a short period of reflection at the end of the day – almost a 'recap' or walking through of your day – can highlight moments when you acted in ways you are not necessarily happy with. We can recognise these, always with non-judging, loving compassion, and begin to see more effectively the triggers that cause us to act in negative ways, and once we know the triggers we can remove them, remove ourselves from the triggers, or simply choose a different course of action in response to the trigger.

Reflection can also provide great material for therapy work – talk therapy, cognitive behavioural therapy, Psych-K etc. As we begin to see some of our personal triggers and the way we respond to them, we can begin to ask the important questions: 'Why do I act this way in this situation?' and 'How does this serve me?' and in doing so find some of our more deep-rooted and limiting self-belief driven behaviours and, most importantly, *change them* over time.

BECOMING CONTENT WITH ACHIEVEMENT

Come to peace with the belief that you can achieve anything your heart desires. The main reason we don't achieve in life is because we don't have the self-belief that we can, and this is predicated by low self-esteem and self-worth.

In your visualisations, notice any feelings of negative self-belief or low self-worth and immediately release them! Imagine always the feeling of ease and power that you have to achieve your goals and let this be a comfort to you.

When you are imagining the moment of achievement or the moments after achieving your goal, feel justifiably proud, allowing contentment to pervade you.

Honour yourself by becoming comfortable with greatness.
Honour yourself by coming to peace with your own
beautiful power.
You are an expression of the divine.

Chapter 8 Exercises

Encourage a daily meditative practice

A basic sitting meditation using mindfulness of breath.

- Find a quiet, comfortable place to sit

- Sit with your back straight and upright, not rigidly but with good posture. You may like to use a traditional posture such as a lotus or half-lotus position or sit on your heels with your knees folded under you. These postures were developed for meditation and are very effective. You can also sit in a comfortable chair with your heels flat on the floor and your back upright, supported by the back of the chair.

- Place your hands together in your lap, palms up.

- Close your eyes – not tightly.

- Begin breathing in and out through your nose. Do not 'try' to breathe deeply or in any fashion; simply breathe comfortably and without effort.

- Begin to notice the sensation of the air passing in and out of your nose. There will be a point or area in your nostrils or on the outside rim where you will feel the breath as it moves in and out.

- Gently bring your attention to this area.

- Keep 'watching' the breath; when your mind wanders, simply bring it back gently to the point where you can feel the breath.

Visualising you

- Remove all distractions – cell phone, television, laptop etc.
- Find a quiet, comfortable place to sit or lie.
- Close your eyes lightly and take a few deep belly breaths.
- Spend a few minutes simply noting the sensation of the breath entering the nostrils.
- After a few minutes begin to think about the person you want to be.
- Allow the various thoughts and images to flood over you; let your mind wander and play with the ideas.
- If you find your mind wandering to other topics, gently return it to the visualisation.

Simply do this for a few minutes. Afterwards close out by returning your attention to the breath and say your personal mantra to yourself.

Write down in a journal any thoughts or ideas that arose in your visualisation. This can be used later to help you formulate goals.

Create a personal mantra

Creating a personal mantra can be a valuable tool in beginning to impress upon our subconscious what we want to be true — which is not always what our subconscious beliefs allow us to actually make true! But through intention and action we can change the way we act and react to stimuli (people, places and situations). Just a few choice words can be a great way to begin to become more and more the person we want to be.

In your visualisation exercise you will have begun to get an idea of the person you want to be and the type of life you want to be living. With this in mind take a few moments to think of just a few — I think three has a nice ring to it — words that encapsulate the most important aspects.

This may change at times, especially if you need to focus on a particular area of your life in order to reach your goals.

I have used a very basic mantra many times in the past. It is:

'I am happy, confident and creative.'

Simple, huh!?

In fact, the beauty of this type of positive reinforcement is in its simplicity. Basic, every-day and yet powerful words can make profound changes in the way we think and act.

The mantra you create can be used as a short exercise any time of the day.

Just close your eyes, relax, breathe and say it to yourself.

It is also a great way to close out meditation or start the day.

When you use your mantra, visualise yourself as those words. For example, when I use my mantra, I might see myself beaming a *huge* smile, laughing, talking with people and having fun, walking confidently into lectures and sitting at my computer typing excitedly a few more chapters of my latest book or article.

If you say it, and if you see it, it will become, more and more.

Reflections

Am I healthy and happy?

Do I speak positively to myself?

Do I frame my affirmations in the present or the future?

Would I benefit from getting some help with my journey?

CHAPTER NINE

Get Your 'Freek' On

How to create abundance in the gift economy

"ONE MUST KNOW NOT JUST HOW TO ACCEPT A GIFT, BUT WITH WHAT GRACE TO SHARE IT."
~ MAYA ANGELOU

It is becoming abundantly clear that the way we do business and the way commerce works is fundamentally changing.

The 'free' model of business is becoming one of the, if not *the* prevailing paradigm of business. The old standard of creating a product, finding a price point and then selling it does not always hold true in an age where many products are offered to the public for free. Some of the most profitable companies in the world (like Google) offer the vast majority of their products at no cost and revenue is generated by monetising systems built *around* the products, particularly advertising.

It has reached a point where any company almost has to make a choice of whether they are going to charge for their products or allow their products to be a gratis vehicle for some other type of monetising system to engender revenue. Either system can work but is certainly has changed the rules by which we buy, sell and live.

A concurrent theme in this new economy is the growth of what has variously been called the 'love' or 'gift' economies.

An increasing amount of time is being spent by people providing either products, or more often services (which have little or no fixed costs) and intellectual property to others for free. In the past bartering was common, but there is a move nowadays towards simply providing services and IP to others, where one's time allows, at no charge, and without any definite or even implied charge. The distinction is important, as barter is still a transaction, whereas the love/gift economies remove the entire question of payment because what is being provided truly is a gift.

There is a very distinct psychological dynamic in the gift/love economy.

We often have a future-focused view of the transaction when we are providing or purchasing services for cash or barter; however, when we are simply providing a service for free, out of love, we are more likely to be 'present' in the moment, because there is no payment that we are looking towards receiving. The act itself is the entire encapsulation of its own being. Without any payment asked for or expected there is no need to be anywhere other than here and now.

One of the struggles that many alternative health practitioners and people involved in the spiritual side of health have – and I have mentored many of them – is asking for payment from their patients and clients. Whilst this can be as a result of negative and ultimately self-limiting and self-defeating beliefs around the value of money and self-worth – which should be worked on – the interesting side-line of the gift economy is that it completely removes this issue.

I have noticed over the years I have become more and more involved in simply helping people out. I treat my friends, I help people who are less fortunate financially, and I give my time and money to various charities. I have often found myself, sometimes to the detriment of my financial health, going above and beyond the call of duty and providing additional help, advice and remedies to my patients without charging. I simply want people to be healthy, well and happy. But I have noticed a peculiar thing happening as a result of this.

The period between late 2007 and late 2009 was financially the worst I have ever been through.

Within this period, I went from virtual semi-retirement and a healthy asset base to living hand to mouth and day to day. There were times when I would fast, meditate and pray simply because I didn't have anything to eat. But as things were getting to their absolute worst a strange thing started happening—patients, clients and friends would randomly call me up and offer to take me out for dinner, or people I'd helped would drop by unexpectedly with gifts of food. It seemed as if, in my moment of greatest need, those whom I had helped in theirs were with me to offer their own gifts of love in return. And it certainly wasn't because they knew of my plight, because it was not common knowledge.

This got me thinking about how much of our economy is based upon this giving and receiving of gifts – and I would hazard a guess that it is a significant amount. There is a huge and largely unaccounted for 'economy' involved with the giving of time and effort with no thought of reward, even when, in reality, there *always* is a payback. This is significant because if you are *earning* a certain dollar amount, this may not accurately reflect what you are actually *receiving*.

Anyone who has been a sponsored athlete will know this. At times I have been supplied with supplements, clothing, equipment and shoes as part of endorsement or sponsorship deals, and this has significantly decreased my expenditure. Likewise, if you are receiving gifts, albeit unrequested, as a result of your own generosity in the past, this may provide a significant boost to your living situation and can make your income level somewhat less than accurate when evaluating the quality of life and quality of time it engenders. But giving to others should not be looked at as a transaction that will eventually be 'paid back'. This leads to inevitable resentment if the party given to doesn't in turn provide something back.

Giving must be done with open hands and an open heart, without forethought of recompense. This frees us from any potential anguish or resentment and allows us to purely enjoy the moment of giving for its own beautiful reward.

We always receive a payment for giving … and that payment is the *payment of love*. When we give, we feel great! That alone should be enough to justify the giving of our time, efforts, possessions and goods to others – where we are able and where it is viable. As our whole modus operandi is to create joyous experiences giving is an easy way to do just that, instantly.

Several companies have taken this concept to its logical, although not always viable, conclusion and have begun to offer their services and/or products simply by donation. Previously the near sole domain of government, philanthropist or trust-backed organisations such as art galleries and museums, payment by donation is now entering mainstream commerce – and not just for informational products and services. Real, tangible goods are being offered for sale at whatever cost the *customer* believes it is worth, or that they can spare.

Ron Shaich, former CEO of Panera Bread, recently reopened a St Louis Panera Bread café as 'non-profit' with a 'pay what you can' model[12]. It remains to be seen whether this venture will be economy viable in the long term. It also remains to be seen whether others will follow suit. However, it

____

[12] St Louis Business Journal Online
http://www.bizjournals.com/stlouis/stories/2010/05/17/daily21.html

is certainly already common for software and other information products to be provided free to the public. Many information products are backed by donations from end users and also by large companies wishing to enhance and maintain visibility. Some are simply provided for free as a counter-culture movement against corporatisation and consumerism, but in any event the low costs of storage and logistics (due to the increasing and already abundant capacity of the internet) have allowed this, and we have in turn benefited.

UTILISING THE FREE ECONOMY

As already stated, when we spend less cash we obviously need to earn less – and, therefore, work less – in order to satisfy our other needs and wants.

A tantalising aspect of the gift economy has been the growth of 'free' (or 'gratis') as a valid set point for business. Whether as a 'lead-in' for paid services or premium products, or as a vehicle for paid advertising, free products and services are becoming more and more popular. And not only are they growing in popularity – as they are always bound to do due to their enticing price point of zero – but they are also fast becoming comparable, if not equally as good as, paid-for products with which they compete.

This is particularly true in the online world of applications and software. This move was originally driven by the open source movement and has been equal parts counterculture expressionism, fluid experimentalism and paradigm-changing pioneering.

Take the obvious example of Google. Google is ranked at 102 on the Fortune 500 list of US largest companies by revenue (with approximate yearly earnings of over 23.6 billion dollars[13]) but its extraordinarily high profit margins place it much higher on profit listings. With earnings only six per cent that of number one listed Walmart, it returns a profit equivalent to 45 per cent of that of the retail giant. The reasons for this are obvious. Walmart and most of the other major players on the Fortune 500 list have huge costs associated with infrastructure, logistics, and human capital, and most importantly, stockholding and purchasing. But bear in mind that Google's profits are built on a model of only two to five per cent of its customers buying anything at all! That means over 95 per cent of its customers (its users) aren't buying anything, and therefore 95 per cent of its business is being offered completely for free. The revenue is being generated solely by the monetising of systems around free products.

There are many other examples of the free model being applied by companies in the areas of software and new media, and precisely because these models are free, the uptake of

---

[13] CNN Money/Fortune Magazine Website -
http://money.cnn.com/magazines/fortune/fortune500/2010/full_list/101_200.htm
l

them is enormous, and they are fast becoming some of the biggest vehicles for social change.

Social networks such as Facebook and Myspace have had enormous impact on the way we communicate and interact with one another, and this has in turn been highly adopted – although seldom effectively – by commercial interests with a resultant paradigm shift in the way marketing, branding and advertising are undertaken.

Information-gathering has been increasingly influenced by the Web and most especially by the blogging movement and social information 'feeders', most obviously Twitter, which has, for many, taken the place of traditional news feeds. These information sources are often touted by those in the traditional media as inherently unreliable. The reality, though, is that there has always been unreliable information. The difference now is that instead of a hand-printed manifesto from someone with a vested interest in an industry, ideology or cause, we now have websites, blogs, Twitter accounts and Facebook pages from which to get the information we desire – whether considered reliable or not. And 'reliable', in practice, is a synonym for 'mainstream'.

Information outside the norm is considered unreliable by nature, but if we believe it to be true, we will seek it out regardless. We now have the ability to find, at a faster rate and with better efficacy, more of the information that is most important to *us*.

This can be a double-edged sword as we can spend more time finding out 'about' things rather than learning more deeply by 'doing', and our time can be overly and overtly diverted. On the other hand, we have the power to do more of what we love, more easily, and increased ability to connect to others with similar interests. We are also in the enviable position of being able to learn about others and break down the barriers of ignorance if we so wish.

How the Free Economy Makes Us Time-Richer

Many products you currently use could potentially be replaced by free alternatives. If you replace a paid-for product by a free one, you are able to realise, immediately, more spending potential for other things and/or reduce the work burden required to satisfy your needs and wants. The key, though, is that the products must not cost any additional time in terms of locating and, most importantly, maintaining them. Educating oneself in their use could also be a time burden that reduces the real gain of the product.

Many people have found that some open source and free software actually costs more to maintain and use, both in money and time, than simply buying a copy of a popular product that comes complete with support and the ability to cheaply upgrade over time. But this is often not true.

I am, for example, writing this book in OpenOffice (www.openoffice.org) – a free, open source competitor to the

Microsoft Office suite. I must admit I do like the latest incarnations of the Microsoft product and I don't find OpenOffice to be quite as good as the latest version of Office; however, for what I need to do it is basically the same, and almost as good, so the difference between the cost of $100–$500, depending on options, and a price point of $0 is very important. When on the road I am able to access all my current files through programmes such as Dropbox (www.dropbox.com) and, if I need to, write and revise documents, spreadsheets and presentations remotely through free Google Docs.

Where there is no discernible benefit to buying a more expensive product, I will always take the cheaper one. That to me is simple common sense.

By utilising existing aspects of the free economy, we can reduce our spending load and thereby increase the amount of both time and money we have to enjoy those joyous experiences that make life worth living.

The free audit

This exercise is an ongoing one. When you have to purchase something – especially a systems-based product, such as software, or something for your business, do a quick internet search for free options.

You will often find there are free or at the very least cheaper options than the standard, industry or 'mainstream' accepted norm.

Useful Free Resources:

File storage

Dropbox

www.dropbox.com

Word processing, spreadsheets and presentations

OpenOffice

www.openoffice.org

Google Docs

www.docs.google.com

Online scheduling

Tungle

www.tungle.me

An example of my scheduling page is at
www.tungle.me/cliffharvey

Splash page
About Me
www.about.me
An example of my personal splash page is at
www.about.me/cliffharvey

Free website design tools
Weebly
www.weebly.com

Wix
www.wix.com

Blogs
Blogger
www.blogger.com
I use Blogger for my mind-body-spirit blog at
www.cliffdog.com

WordPress
www.wordpress.com

Microblogs

Tumblr

www.tumblr.com

Example (I love Tumblr)

www.cliffharvey.tumblr.com

Posterous

www.posterous.com

Social networking management

HootSuite

www.hootsuite.com

TweetDeck

www.tweetdeck.com

Note: These are simply some of my favourites, all of which I have used. Products and offerings also change over time. Caveat emptor always applies.

Reflections

Do I give freely, or expecting something in return?

*Do I get annoyed or angered if I give something and receive
no payment 'in kind' or otherwise?*

*Are there ways I could utilise the 'free economy' to give
myself the gift of time?*

CHAPTER TEN

Happiness Now

Why being happy makes you happy

"I, NOT EVENTS, HAVE THE POWER TO MAKE ME HAPPY OR UNHAPPY TODAY. I CAN CHOOSE WHICH IT SHALL BE."
~ GROUCHO MARX

The happiness we derive from life is to a large degree learned.

Happiness is an intrinsic state, not something that occurs spontaneously as a result of what occurs around us, or what windfalls befall us. Likewise, unhappiness is a result of our relationship with the world around us. Therefore, it rests on a foundation of what we fundamentally believe to be true.

We can learn to be happy, and we can learn over time to become happier and happier. It is our relationship with stimuli that determines how we will feel about it. The stimuli themselves don't promote an inevitable and intractable emotion.

This concept can be very disconcerting for people. When we so often think it is external events that 'cause' our happiness, it is extremely challenging to change our mindset to one where we are in the driving seat of our happiness. It compels action, and action is seldom welcomed if we feel victimised by circumstance and are wallowing in our malaise. But conversely there is enormous opportunity and inspiration in our own ability to begin to choose to live a happier life, day to day.

We can see this in action when different people respond in entirely different ways to the same situation, person or scenario. One person may be extremely stressed out due to an interaction with a certain difficult personality, but for another person dealing with the same difficult dynamic there is no stress. It's like 'water off a duck's back' – they simply aren't bothered by it. If emotions, thoughts and feelings were dictated by outside circumstances the reactions of these two people would be more or less the same. The way the person *relates* to a situation determines how they, in turn, *think* and *feel* about it.

And much of the way we relate to situations is based upon our past conditioning. This can begin at the moment we are conceived (and in all likelihood earlier – but I digress) and not just from our moment of birth (showing the importance of 'conscious pregnancy') and continues right through to the present moment. This conditioning may also include both genetic imperatives, received from our parents and ancestors and also from the karmic and energetic effects of past lives. This conditioning to action creates much of the way we react subconsciously to the things we see and experience around us. When we become aware of our actions – primarily as a result of becoming more mindful – we can begin to see whether these 'reactions' are helping us to live the life we want to be living, or not. We can then go about creating change, and change is indeed very possible.

The Neurophysiology of Happiness

Anything we 'do' – movement, thought, speech and even emotion – has a neurological basis. There are neural pathways responsible for anything we actively or subconsciously do. These neural pathways are the links between all the neurons in the brain that initiate and co-ordinate anything that happens within the body. The interesting thing is that, although there are general areas of the brain associated with certain things (like hearing or speech, for example), these areas are actually different for all of us, albeit extremely subtly, and so previous distinctions of brain areas related to specific functions which are more or less unchangeable are not wholly correct.

There are many examples of people who, having suffered a traumatic brain injury, are able to create new neural pathways to compensate for the damage to existing pathways responsible for various senses and skills. The brain literally changes its very anatomy and physiology in response to the conditioning we place upon it.

This has fascinating implications for learning.

In one of my former roles as a strength coach for elite athletes I saw in practice that the neural basis of movement and skills learning has made, and still is making a big impact on strength and conditioning for athletes. While most people think strength is related to gross muscular physiology, it is plainly evident that due to its neural basis it is actually more a consequence of neuro-muscular patterning[14]. And, like strength development or complex skills learning, happiness is also to a large degree *learned*.

This concept seems counter-intuitive to many, and indeed its implications are quite challenging. Happiness, after all, seems to be something that occurs as a result of things that happen to us, not something that we 'do'. But it really is something that we *do*. Happiness is dependent upon how we respond and adapt to stimuli over time, rather than simply being a blind reaction to it.

If we create greater and greater moments of, and longer periods of happiness in our lives we literally begin to create a brain – and more correctly a mind-body complex – that is more efficient at being happy, and conversely less efficient at being depressed. Of course, we will all get down at times, but when we are happier this becomes our more natural 'set point'.

By developing a higher normal and appropriate set point of happiness (in other words being more generally happy more

---

[14] http://cliffdog.blogspot.com/2009/11/training-movements-not-muscles.html

of the time) we are able to live happier lives and are able to be more resistant to calamity, that previously may have sent us into a depressive spiral.

A very cool adjunct to this is that when, for example, we smile, we initiate the release of a cascade of hormones and neurotransmitters that are responsible for happiness. It has even been said that *perhaps we don't so much smile because we are happy, but we are happy because we smile!*

This release of 'happiness chemicals' encourages the neurophysiological changes that develop stronger neural pathways associated with happiness, which become further strengthened the more moments of happiness and joy we have. So not only can we have fleeting moments of connective happiness with people, places and events, but through these we can actually become generally happier people. We really can change our physiology to become happier.

Note: I highly recommend reading *The Brain That Changes Itself* by Norman Doidge, *Molecules of Emotion* by Candace Pert and *The Biology of Belief* by Bruce Lipton.

Get into the habit of smiling. We know that smiling actually makes us happier, and we can measure the real physiological causes and effects of this. Therefore, it is not just wishful thinking; it's hard, concrete science.

But don't just smile in response to things – develop a 'self-smile' – a small, almost imperceptible smile that you wear all day long. Let's face it — if you aren't angry, unhappy or depressed for a defined reason, your set point might as well be happiness … and it can be. We co-create our reality, so we can decide that being happy will more and more become our natural state of being.

It can be hard to smile though; but here's an easy exercise to help it along:

Stop, breathe and relax.

Now close your eyes gently.

With your eyes closed picture your face. See it clearly in your mind's eye. See every line and contour. Conjure up the image of *your* face, as it is right now. And now with that image in your mind's eye, imagine the face — your face — smiling. Watch as a *big* smile spreads out from the corners of your mouth and envelops your whole face. Picture you with your true, spontaneous, beaming, beautiful smile. The *biggest* smile you have ever had in fact!

What happened?

I bet you ended up smiling, not just in your mind's eye, but in reality, too.

I have performed this exercise countless times in lectures and workshops, and I have yet to find a single person who didn't smile as a result of this valuable exercise.

Take a brief moment to think about what just happened; you visualised *you* smiling and being happy. That visualisation was an *intention* that created a reality of you smiling, and when you smile you become happier, even if just for a brief moment, but that brief moment is *training* you to become happier by nature. Like anything else, if we repeat something over and over again, we become more proficient at it, and it becomes more natural. Being happy is no different.

When you are going about your daily activities, if you happen to catch someone's eye, instead of looking away – smile.

Even a brief smile helps to make someone else feel that little bit better. When someone smiles at you what do you inevitably do? You smile a little as well and if, in that moment, someone else catches you smiling what do they do? They smile as well. And so, this cascade of smiles creates a ripple effect of joy and happiness. This could in reality encircle the globe and make every single person on the planet a little bit happier. And consider that if we continue to do this and create more moments of happiness, our level of happiness will continue to rise, as will the people we affect, and the people they affect, and the world's entire vibration of positivity will continue to rise.

I was discussing this concept with my dad. He asked me if I really thought I could change the world by such simple actions as smiling, laughing and opening up to people on a day-to-day and moment-to-moment basis, to which I replied, "Of course!"

You see, there are many things we *could* do on some grand scale to help make the world a better place. We could travel to Africa and build schools for the poor; we could start campaigns for women's literacy in countries where a woman's value is under appreciated; we could campaign for all manner of causes we believe in. I love activism, and I am involved in many causes, but whether you are involved or not, there are simple, daily, momentary actions you can do, with little to *no* effect on your time, money or energy, that can promote greater peace, love and joy in the world. So the question is: 'If you can do these things so easily, then why wouldn't you?', and I believe these small actions done by more of us could actually have the greatest effect on changing our lives, the lives of those around us and the world, for the better.

BECOME A CONNECTOR
GIVING THE GIFT OF *YOU* TO OTHERS

I am amazed and fascinated when I walk to work in the morning – yes, I walk to work – that most everyone I pass seems so absolutely disconnected from everyone else. Not only that, but they seem completely disconnected from the world around them. Walking with their heads down, hooked up to their iPods and media players, shuffling off to work wrapped in their own thoughts. Of course, there is nothing wrong with being wrapped in your own thoughts but notice when you inadvertently (or purposely) catch someone's eye; the usual response is for most people, most of the time, to look away, avoiding eye contact at all costs.

Whatever happened to us, that the mere thought of opening oneself, even if only for a moment, to another human was something to be avoided, and even more alarming, something to be scared of?

Many will say that we live in a dangerous world, that violent crime is not a rare occurrence, and that the mere thought of inviting a stranger into our lives in any small way, even if only for the briefest of moments with a glance and a smile, is cavalier at best and dangerous at worst. But in spite of any perceived danger, our fear of connection has made us less open to joyous experience. After all, it is connection with others that provides the greatest experiences in life. Interpersonal dynamics and meaningful interpersonal relationships are the ultimate expression of love and joy.

This is why many of us want to find a life partner – because this provides the deepest level of connection, something that cannot be accomplished with the breadth of experiences that come from a myriad of skin-deep acquaintances with people. True friendships, too, are a deep, meaningful connection and provide a fantastic example of why connection is so important. Imagine life without it.

Connection is absolutely crucial for our well-being. It has been theorised that one of the primary reasons for the phenomena of road rage, for example, is disconnection. Researchers have found that the longer people are isolated in their cars, the greater the rate of road rage incidents. It is thought we lose our rationality and our framework for social interaction when we are isolated from others for extended periods of time.

I think, too, that this lack of connection results in more violence and hatred. After all, it is hard to hate a person if you have developed a meaningful and loving connection with them, and by extension it is almost impossible to hate a group of people if you have had a meaningful and loving connection with a person from that group. It is ignorance that leads to xenophobia, homophobia, racism and bigotry. Ignorance of the people that are members of a group runs counter to the understanding that we share so much more in *common* with them, than all of our differences combined.

With greater connection with the people around us, we can see that people are all inherently good on some level, even if it is only a kernel hidden deep under layers of anger, greed or hate. We can also see ourselves in those people, even if only in some small way, and we can empathise with, relate to and eventually find ourselves loving all for our shared humanity. The vast similarities between each and every one of us shine through, and we see so much of ourselves in others that it becomes impossible to carry on the cycle of hate.

An interesting example is mentioned in *Power vs. Force: The Hidden Determinants of Human Behavior* by David Hawkins. Using applied muscle testing, researchers in the field of applied kinesiology are able to test subconscious belief patterns. The author notes that almost across the board people test 'strong' when exposed to images of people such as Martin Luther King, Jr and Mahatma Ghandi, and 'weak' when exposed to images of people considered archetypes of evil, such as Adolf Hitler. This would appear obvious, but what is most surprising is that neo-Nazis and self-identified racists who were tested, in spite of their conscious feelings about the figures shown, still tested positive to the humanitarian leaders and negative to the despots and tyrants. This example shows that perhaps there really is a kernel of goodness and wholeness within each of us, and elements of humanity that, although hidden, are consciously still there.

By connecting even with those we are not necessarily enamoured with, for whatever reason, we honour this principle.

'… listen to others, even to the dull and the ignorant; they too have their story …'

~ from 'The Desiderata' by Max Ehrmann

VIRTUOUS HAPPINESS

With connection we can begin to act in a eudaemonistic fashion to create 'virtuous happiness'. We can begin to act in ways that are leading to greater connection with people, greater amounts of joyous experience and an overall elevation in the happiness not just of ourselves but the people around us.

1.   Enjoy Traffic

We have all had that sinking feeling in the pit of our stomach when we pull on to the motorway and see gridlock, with cars stretched out motionless for miles ahead of us. But if we think about it, it is our aversion to sitting in traffic that is a problem. The traffic really is inconsequential. Of course, sometimes we are in a rush to get somewhere, and we become extremely frustrated by not being able to get there on time – or at all. But in these cases, we have to make one of two choices: a) remain frustrated and get inevitably more so, or b) let it go. The traffic will not suddenly clear because we want it to, and the only thing we accomplish by getting angry is to waste our precious time on a needless emotional void.

I used to drive to work every day (I now work mainly from home). At the time my business was located across the other side of town, and I inevitably spent at least two hours in my car every day – something the environmentalist in me would not do now. I was at first frustrated by this, and every morning I would have an inevitable sense of foreboding as I neared the motorway and a sinking feeling when I saw the cars lined up in their droves, heading off to their workplaces.

But over time a realisation began to dawn on me.

I was very busy building my fledgling practice as well as a nutritional supplement business, and when I factored in training and spending time with my friends, family and girlfriend I had very little time to myself.

The time I was spending in traffic was the single biggest amount of 'alone time' I had in any given day. It took up more of my day than either reading, meditation, or my physical training. I actually realised that although I had a large amount of aversion to being in traffic, on many levels I actually enjoyed it. I did a lot of mental planning, I listened to music, sang along and listened to spoken word comedy and had a great laugh. I even spent a lot of my 'in-car' time performing daily mindfulness activities. I was actually spending this time doing things I would otherwise *really* enjoy!

When I understood this, it changed my entire perception of my time in the car. I stopped disliking it and began to simply accept it for what it was.

I took this one step further when I decided that being in traffic was a fantastic opportunity to be kind to others.

I had noticed that in their haste to get wherever they were going people became very selfish and rude. Not letting people in when on-ramps joined the road, not slowing down to let someone change lanes – even speeding up to stop them, in many cases – and all for what?

To be one car space closer to their destination?

The net gain in time to destination just didn't seem worth the negativity brought into my life by being obnoxious.

I made a conscious effort then, and still do now, to be the most courteous and kind person on the road that I can possibly be. I let people in, I slow down to let them merge, I acknowledge their kindness with a wave and, most importantly, if someone else is rude to me, or doesn't help me out, I let it go! The sense of peace and calm that results is worth any amount of effort. Use traffic and other 'inconvenient moments' as a chance to be kind.

Breathe, smile and let go.

Perform small random acts of kindness by letting people in in front of you, giving them a wave and providing an air of positive energy that can be infused into their day and yours.

2.   The gentle art of shopping

It seems that in the modern world, each of us, every day, buys something. From daily coffee to a gas purchase at the service station, to a light lunch, we enter into a monetary transaction with another person, and it is so much more than purely a financial one, though. Every time we make a purchase we are entering into a relationship, an interpersonal dynamic, that although fleeting can be a beautiful and joyous experience. And why shouldn't it be? Even the most fleeting moments can be a chance to improve our lives and that of others.

Think about the last time you went shopping. Were you connected to the experience? Were you connected to the people and the world around you, or were you intentionally disconnecting?

I noticed a strange thing when I was grocery shopping some years ago. The cashiers and the people buying things in line ahead of me were more often than not avoiding making eye contact with each other.

Since then I have observed this time and time again, and it is much more profound at the bigger grocery stores and department stores. At your typical 'mom and pop' store or small coffee house the owner/operators are much more likely to connect, and the 'human element' is still involved in the shopping experience.

Notice next time you are in the supermarket and you get your change back from the cashier, I'll bet that you look at the money being handed back to you, say thank you, collect your shopping bags and hurry out without ever making any sort of connection with the cashier, even if only eye contact.

Is that a bad thing?

No.

But there *is* an opportunity to increase happiness and joy through connection at many junctures in life – and this is one of them.

Next time you are shopping at the supermarket make a conscious effort to look the cashier in the face and say hello when you first arrive at the checkout. When you have purchased your goods look them in the eye, smile, say 'Thank you' and mean it.

I do this religiously and, if nothing else, it makes me feel better. We are human after all, not automatons. It is the interpersonal dynamics that make this life what it is, and it is the interpersonal dynamic of connection that drives our sense of community and plays a major role in our sense of grounding in this life, and by extension, it is one of the crucial co-factors in our ability to lead a positive and happy life.

I can see, repeatedly, by a glimmer in the eye or the smile that spreads across someone's lips, that it is not just me who feels better as a result of this fleeting establishment of connection, but the other party too – and I'm willing to bet it carries on down the line (excuse the pun) to increase the connection and positivity of others.

3.   Put yourself in someone else's shoes

Over the years, the more I started connecting with others, the more I also began to empathise with them. I had always been empathetic and as a child had a huge compulsion towards what I considered to be natural justice, basic human rights and social equity, and this was enhanced by creating greater levels of day-to-day connection with others.

I notice now as I walk down the street, that I recognise people to a depth I hadn't before. It's almost as if rather than simply seeing someone coming towards me, I actually 'become' them for a brief moment and feel their pain, their hurt and their fears and insecurities. In this place it is impossible not to feel empathy and compassion for them.

This wasn't always the case though.

I found it easy to connect with attractive, 'acceptable', 'normal' people, but at times, and in spite of my own sense of natural justice, I would recoil from connecting with those I didn't find attractive or those who scared me in some way.

It is much easier to want to connect with someone you find attractive, and not just in a physical or romantic sense, but those we feel may serve our needs in some way. This is of course born of ego, and of our desire to acquire and possess things. If we only want to connect with people we find attractive, it can be because we want to acquire them as a 'conquest' or as a partner, or because by associating with them we too will be deemed to be attractive, and we may gain some enhancement of social standing from the interaction which therefore reinforces the basis of our insecurities and fears.

On the other hand, our ego-based mindset sees little to gain from connecting with the 'ugly', the homeless and the physically and mentally challenged.

Luckily my sense of natural justice was appalled at my own disconnection from those who may be the most in need of a smile, a kind word and an interaction of non-judgmental love. When I found myself turning away from others it actually disgusted me as it just didn't seem 'fair'.

The goal of connecting is not to get something out of the interaction in the future and it is not to boost one's ego. It is a pure 'in the moment' experience that raises the amount of love and joy in our immediate world. It also has strong flow-on effects – but not necessarily for you straight away and not for your ego-based sense of self.

Because of this realisation that I wanted to attach myself to good-looking people and detach myself from others, I began to wonder why this was, and in doing so put myself in the shoes of the people I wanted to disconnect from. The more this happened, the more I would begin to actually live briefly in their shoes. I would see someone walking towards me and for a brief second, I was almost transported into their body, and as strange as it sounds, I could feel their emotions in that moment and was vividly aware of their pain, trauma and fears and insecurities. When we experience this, it is *impossible* to not be empathic towards that person.

Now this could very well just be profound empathy, but whether it is that or something more, it is good nonetheless, as it allowed me to 'be' the people from whom I had run before. It is connection that can allow us to break down the barriers of ignorance, and by better empathising with and knowing people we were previously detached from, we can instead begin to love them as vital and important human beings – who are pretty much just the same as us.

We are, after all, more or less the same.

As human animals we are all more or less the same. We so often think of our individuality and our own personal rights and freedoms, and we cling to these concepts so tightly that we forget that genetically, physically, emotionally and spiritually we are all very much the same.

Even a chimpanzee shares over 98.4 per cent of its genetic material with us, so we are not too dissimilar from monkeys either. And we are virtually identical to everyone else on the planet in spite of how different we look.

Sure, we feel things slightly differently; we have slightly different reactions to situations. We are all conditioned to behave differently to events based on our conditioning, based upon everything we have ever experienced and been exposed to in our lives; but fundamentally these are all nuances of the common human experience. We all feel pain; we all feel hurt, hunger, joy and love. These are common to all of us.

How on earth can we dismiss, harm, cheat and steal from those around us who are nearly identical?

It is a slight cliché but what a truism there is in the Judaeo-Christian concept of 'doing unto others as you would have them do unto you'. In fact, if you really consider the effect your actions have on those around you, and if you contemplate and reflect on what it is like to be hurt by someone and relate that to the experience of one of our fellow humans, it is even harder to do.

On a universal level if we imagine we are all interconnected, we can take this concept one step further: By doing unto others as you would have them do unto you, you are in fact doing unto yourself.

We all experience the gamut of human emotions and experience in slightly different ways. But we are also all connected by our shared heritage in greater circles of association.

As I discussed in my book *Choosing You!* much of the way we act, think and feel is determined by our upbringing and all the many and varied things – sights, sounds, interactions, media – we have been exposed to during our lives. But in addition to this we are also influenced by the genetic material passed on to us by our forebears, which was in turn influenced by the conditions that affected those forebears. So, there is a totality of our own heritage that affects us.

But wait …there's more.

We are also, in small ways, affected by everything else in the world. We like to think we are individual and sovereign, but in fact we are in many ways merely constructs of our own devising. Our body, for example, appears to us at any moment to be solid and distinct in nature. But of course, it is constantly changing; it is constantly regenerating itself.

The majority of cells within your body will be replaced within months, and at any given time your body is, apart from a few enduring cells, under 10 years old.

And where does the material come from to create these cells?

From the food we eat.

So, we are absorbing from the world around us in order to change ourselves.

Further, the 'intention' to create these cells and to configure them comes from our belief-based patterning, so we provide both the chemical building blocks as well as the pattern.

We literally co-create ourselves and our reality through our own action and intention.

On a more micro scale we are *constantly* gaining and losing matter and energy. What we deem to be solid and defined is really only so because of our perception.

We perceive ourselves to be defined when in fact if we changed our reference point of perception we would not be anywhere near so. Look at it this way: If I were to run into you, we would either stop dead or one of us would fall over; however, if I were an X-ray, I would simply pass through you unimpeded.

The world is more of a 'flow' than a 'thing'. It is a constant interchange of energy and matter where everything that happens affects everything else in the world and in the universe by smaller and smaller degrees. This 'ripple effect' of action and consequence has the power to literally change the world and the universe and the way that we perceive it functions.

Your World in Five Metres: Creating a Bubble of Happiness!

We are constantly bombarded by stimuli, and these stimuli (or more correctly our relationship with those stimuli) have a massive effect on the way we think, act and feel. Our environment affects our level of happiness on a grand scale. For this reason, it is important to make sure our environment is conducive to happiness.

We can choose to have a happy environment. We can create what I like to call a 'five-metre happiness bubble' around us that is overwhelmingly positive. Those who come into this sphere are affected by our connecting with them and are subtly affected by the energy of positivity that we create.

On my walk to work in the morning I pass a lot of people. I could choose not to look people in the eye but to look down at the ground and ignore them. But this would only serve to increase the disconnection we have with our fellow man.

So, I *choose* to look people in the eye, to smile and perhaps even say a hearty 'Good morning!' And here's the coolest part – whenever I smile at someone they almost always smile back! And inevitably they end up smiling at someone else, who also smiles back ... and so it goes on. By one simple action we have elevated another person's level of happiness if only for a moment. But more than that, we have started a cascade of incrementally elevating happiness by initiating a chain of events in a sequence potentially without an end! That in itself is a powerful thing and a fantastic example of how small actions can have big effects. I can't help but think if more people took on this tiny idea the consequences for our total happiness on earth would go up significantly, with profound consequences for world peace and understanding.

Is this a tad utopian?

Perhaps; but even if I only serve to make my day and someone else's happier, it is still *well* worth it.

It can be hard, I know, to connect with people and to let people who are potentially grumpy, mean or nasty into our lives, even for a brief second. But remember everyone has a kernel of goodness, a kernel of truth and love within them. It is their very humanity, and like a kernel in nature's kingdom, when nurtured in the right way it can blossom and begin to break through the exterior of hurt, shame and embarrassment that has become a cloak we create in response to the trauma and hurt in the world around us.

When I feel like giving up and simply withdrawing into my shell, creating disconnection, and if I become despondent about the hate, greed and narcissism we can all too readily see in the world around us, I like to remember these timeless words:

'Be kind — for everyone you meet is fighting a great battle …'
~ Philo

I can't remember exactly where I first saw this quote – I think it may have been in one of Lama Surya Das's books – in any case, it had and continues to have a profound effect on me. Often the simplest words ring the truest.

We are so quick to judge and vilify those whose actions we see as negative, annoying or 'wrong', and we are also just as quick to forget the times that perhaps we have been in that very same situation.

I'm sure most of us, most of the time, try our best to live a good life of warmth and charity. But we all slip up from time to time. We can never know exactly what another person is going through, what hardships they are facing, or have already faced, but we can be empathetic to their plight and do one simple thing – be kind.

There is no excuse for people to act poorly, as I said in *Choosing You! 'There are reasons for the way people act – not excuses.'*

In seeing the reasons why people sometimes act rashly or negatively, but not necessarily excusing them we are being kind. We can treat them with gentleness, openness and love. These things are the basis of compassion.

Philo's timeless quote wells into my mind when I am reactively disgusted by someone, by the way they act or look, and it immediately disarms these negative thoughts – and as simply as they arose, they faded away to be replaced by feelings of love and compassion for my fellow man.

Words can hold so much power. They say that *'God is in*

the word'. For me this means there is power and truth in words. What we say becomes real and what is said to us affects the co-creation of our reality.

Remember that simply being kind – for everyone you meet is fighting a great battle – is also perhaps the greatest exercise in charity.

The stimuli fast

This is a great exercise to begin to reconnect with the people and the world around you. Often, we use distractions to fill our time when we don't know (that is, we haven't thought about) what we *really* want to be doing.

We also use various means of distraction to make it easier *not* to communicate and connect with those around us. Consider this example:

On the bus most people do one of two things – they listen to a portable music device (iPod or MP3 player) or they read something (a newspaper, magazine or book). If you use public transport you will have seen this. If you don't take public transport, take a bus and check out how many people are distracting themselves with some form of media.

I am not saying that this is in any way bad. I use the bus and it can be a great place to read and to catch up on research for my writing and my health practice. And because I love music, I love the chance to listen to some of my favourite bands. But there is an interesting side note to this: when we are in relatively close confines with other people there is a general level of discomfort. Researchers have noted that many modern situations put us in a proximity to others that we do not naturally enjoy and because of this we have a tendency to create disconnection.

Consider another example:

You enter an elevator. Do you a) face the person next to you, or b) face the door? The answer of course is inevitably b). Not only do we not face others, we purposely avoid eye contact, and if contact takes place inadvertently, we break it almost immediately. The subtle issue of safety also rears its head as we don't want to invite contact with the unknown. They might be psychopaths, after all.

However, the vast majority of people are good, and all of us have a kernel of pure goodness – even if it is extremely well hidden. A degree of connection with people – by a smile, a hello or simply making eye contact – could even be enough to help someone connect with their own goodness. Disconnection can be one of the contributing factors in creating sociopathic behaviour in otherwise normal people.

Don't consume any information that isn't necessary, for an entire weekend

This means not reading books, magazines, newspapers or journals. It also means not watching television or surfing the Web.

Finally – and maybe the hardest – it also means not listening to music, especially on your MP3 player.

There is nothing wrong with any of these activities. Listening to music is richly rewarding. We learn, revel and 'play' mentally when we read books, and we find information we need when we read magazines, journals or surf the Net. But often these things are used merely as time-filling distractions.

They allow us to inadvertently turn off to the people and things around us. There can be a real world of wonder just around the corner when we decide to merely 'be' instead of plugging in to our iPod when we walk out of the house.

We hear the birds chirping, the rustle of the leaves and the sound of rain on a tin roof – all those things that begin to connect us to the world around us. We hear the voices of others, the laugh of a baby, and we also begin to notice more with our other senses too. By removing the bubble of stimulus that we wrap ourselves in, we are allowed to stop and smell the roses – literally if need be!

So – just for one weekend – remove the iPod, ignore the magazines, books and television and simply focus on a few days of pure connection. Focus on breathing, relaxing, being mindful of the sights, sounds, smells and tastes of the world around you. Revel once again in the wonder and joy of this beautiful earth we live on and appreciate the people you come into contact within this small part of your life's journey.

Reflections

Is my 'natural' face a frown or a smile?

Could I smile more?

Do I make and maintain contact with others or break it?

Am I kind to others? (Think deeply about that one)

Am I kind and gentle to myself?

CHAPTER ELEVEN

Selflessness & Charity

Realising the joy in giving

"DOWN IN THEIR HEARTS, WISE MEN KNOW
THIS TRUTH: THE ONLY WAY TO HELP
YOURSELF IS TO HELP OTHERS."
~ ELBERT HUBBARD

We have all felt the joy of giving. When we make someone happy by giving them a gift we receive as much if not more joy from that act. When we give to someone who is really in need, and when we can improve the length or quality of their life, the joy that action creates is immeasurable.

This not only serves to make us happy in the moment of giving, but in the long run as well, as I'm sure it helps to create a more conducive 'field' of happiness in the world.

Many social and economic theorists consider there are 'tipping points' when actions and behaviours, when committed by enough people, become the rule rather than the exception. Not only could this be true with the act of giving itself – and the move towards a gift or love-based economy is a tantalising prospect – but also in the action of happiness itself.

If more people are happy there will be a greater general impetus for happiness within society. We will simply be conditioned to a higher, more joyful neural 'set-point'.

Giving really does help create this field of joy and hope, and in a way that will feed back to us over and over again and continue to raise the levels of planetary happiness. More than ever we are beginning to realise the interconnectedness of us all. Our actions affect the health, and well-being of every other person on the planet; but more than this, our actions affect the wellness and growth, in a holistic sense, of every other being on the planet and every other 'thing' in the universe. When we realise this interconnectedness, the way we treat each other, and the way we treat the planet, begins to look very nonsensical.

As ecologist Joanna Macy puts it:

"The obvious choice is to extend our notions of self-interest. For example, it would not occur to me to plead with you, 'Oh, don't saw off your leg. That would be an act of violence.' It wouldn't occur to me because your leg is part of your body. Well so are the trees in the Amazon rain basin. They are our external lungs. And we are beginning to realize that the world is our body."

We have – for the greatest portion of our existence as a human species, and in the greatest critical mass of our actions

– been in a paradigm of *taking*. This paradigm has been characterised by taking from one another, taking from the planet and keeping what we can for ourselves at the expense of all else. One of the ways in which we will not only *survive* but *thrive* as humanity will be to replace this paradigm with one of *giving*. Within a giving paradigm we would instead support each other, support the planet and *give* without expecting a transactional return. We need this change not only to focus on saving the planet, but to foster our own spiritual growth and development ... and yes ... our own happiness.

Peter Singer's book *The Life You Can Save* and its associated website and 'pledge' (where people pledge to donate a donate on an ongoing basis a very small percentage of their income to ameliorate world poverty) provides an easy calculator outlining how much each of us needs to give in order to eliminate extremes of world poverty.

In the lower income brackets this is as little as **one per cent** of your total income. Any of us could certainly afford to give that to people in need, and if we all did that the concept of people in genuine need could cease to exist.

Unfortunately, there is a growing disparity between the rich and poor. This is a cycle seen repeated through history, from the days of chiefdoms, fiefdoms and serfdoms through to the explosion of empires and colonialism. With the uptake of both our modern liberal democracy and moderate socialism through revolution and upheaval, there has been a natural righting of imbalances over time. But lately there is much evidence that the richest within society are becoming disproportionately wealthy.

There also seems to be so much that needs to change – like the very structure of our western financial system – that it is hard to see that this will happen through changing the architecture of our existing society, but will only occur through an active, conscious shift away from materialism.

The Egalitarian Myth of Capitalism

It is considered by many in our Western world that capitalism provides for a form of egalitarianism, in that anyone in a free, modern, democratic society has the same opportunities, and therefore what one *has* is proportionately related to their own efforts, and anyone, in turn, can improve their circumstances by their own efforts. Whilst I don't fully dispute this, and I do think that anyone can improve their circumstances through their own efforts, it is not such a simple equation as Effort = Reward.

There are elements of social prejudice and social privilege that play a major role in the creation and retention of wealth in society, and this automatically excludes the vain notion that equal work will lead to equal reward. While I have been criticised by some on the political right for being 'utopian' in my world view – particularly in my spiritual and holistic world view – these very same critics often from the right of the political spectrum are equally guilty of espousing a utopian – and in this case, I believe, flawed – political world view.

A eudaemonistic view of taxation

I was, for a long time, in favour of a flat tax rate. I considered that a flat tax was the fairest because everyone paid, proportionate to their income, the same relative amount as their contribution to society.

I no longer believe this.

The major change came as a result of several studies that showed a critical tipping point where happiness increased up to a level of income but didn't further increase with additional increases in income. Once people's needs are met and there is a minimal level of 'creature comfort' and security, happiness indicators do not improve.

Let's say, for argument's sake, that people earning under $30,000 a year are less happy than those earning over that amount, and further, that as people approach $30,000 per year they become happier, but do not continue to become more-so as they earn 35, 40, 50, 100 or 200,000 dollars per year. This to me shows that if we want to live in a society that is at its absolute best, a society that truly cares for its citizens, that takes its citizens happiness as something of primary importance, then the benchmark of *happiness* should be an important indicator for policy.

In this hypothetical scenario I would propose that there should be *no* tax up to $30,000 per year and that tax should then be graduated, as it currently is, in proportion to someone's income. This way more people, at least those working, would have the greatest opportunity to live happily. This argument could be taken further to encourage minimum wage levels that are more conducive to happiness and not just 'survival' in the most meagre sense of the word.

I often hear the argument, "Why should I pay more because I work harder and improve my position?", and while this argument is in some ways valid, it is also flawed for the following reasons:

The highest earners in society do not necessarily work harder than others. Can you honestly say that an executive earning $200,000 per year works harder than a single mother working two jobs to support her kids at $12 per hour? I would say not.

High earners are not necessarily more productive than others. In fact, I would say that in many cases the productivity per dollar is considerably lower. We see a glaring example of this in law firms where first- and second-year associates provide the greatest return on output (salary) as their productivity is proportionately higher than their salary amount.

Often high salaries, bonuses and executive incentives are given in the presence of losses and/or poor investor and shareholder return. Meaning that it has become a culture of largesse – not one of reward for value, which of course is truly anti-capitalistic. This has also served to strip small investors of their wealth, which has been siphoned away to executive pay and perks.

Salaries of executives have grown disproportionately to all other workers. Take for example CEO pay which was approximately 42 times higher than non-management workers in 1982, rising to 107 times higher in 1990, to the 2000s where it fluctuated between 300 and 500 times what an average worker makes[15].

I have also heard it said that exorbitant and increasing executive pay is related to the level of 'responsibility'. This argument equates high earnings with an implied burden of managing the economic machinery of society. And I do agree with this in part, but if we are less enamoured with attachment to outcomes, and if we begin to see the machinery of society as being the tools with which we 'live' not society itself, the burden of responsibility (equated with stress) becomes markedly reduced. And is the burden of responsibility really that much greater than that carried by the average worker?

Is the burden of responsibility or stress of the position 500 times more than that of the average worker?

---

[15] CNN Money Website
http://money.cnn.com/2005/08/26/news/economy/ceo_pay/

If, as is often stated, executives are smarter or more capable than others, then shouldn't that mitigate the burden they are under? Isn't it, in this sense, relative?

I don't begrudge high salaries to executives. In fact, I applaud it. But I don't agree with the exorbitant salaries now paid out to many, especially where this has drastically outstripped the earnings of middle management and workers.

Stress?

Is being a high-salaried executive more stressful than being one step away from the breadline?

We could all have different opinions on this, but I can tell you that in my experience it's not; however, the self-imposed stress of being caught up in the materialist money game is a very real problem.

There also seems to be a real sense of entitlement of "I worked hard for this so why don't other people?" Hey – here's a freakin' wake-up call … people are working hard, and some of them, but not all, are becoming wealthy. Some of them don't have the same connections or the right skin colour or background to maximally encourage their rising up the ladder which many claim is so easy to climb.

If you are white, male and middle or upper class, you cannot claim your wealth is built purely on the sweat off your own back, because there may well have been women, the poor and ethnic minorities who were working as hard, or harder, than you who were overlooked – for your benefit.

There has always been an upper class and lower class. In some countries – like the new world economies of the United States, Canada, Australia and New Zealand – society has been seen as more egalitarian. But that is changing.

Since the Second World War there has been an increasing consolidation of wealth in the hands of fewer and fewer people in these countries. Increasing wealth in fewer hands increases relative poverty.

Think of it this way – if there is a finite amount of money in an economy, and more of it is controlled by fewer people, there is simply less to go around for the rest.

Again taking a eudaemonistic viewpoint: If this means that more people live below the level of income required for happiness, then this society is not working for the greatest good of its people, and by extension is not working in its own highest good, as we are all part of the greater whole and our health/happiness affects that of the whole and everyone else within it.

Charity and giving are keys to reversing some of the disparities we see, and it begins with a decision we can all make to be less caught up in what we have and more concerned with what we *all* have. It is simply not fair that the wealth of the richest nations is predicated on that of the poorest and that the wealth of the richest individuals in society is, in turn, predicated, again, on that of the poorest.

As we have seen, it is theorised that merely giving one per cent of your income could alleviate the most extreme forms of poverty, so why not give one per cent of what you earn each pay period to a charity?

It could be the same charity every month or week, or you could pick and choose on a whim. There are many worthy charities out there, and less important than how much we give or who we give to, is that we *are* in fact giving to people in need.

Here are just a few of the worthy charities that you may want to donate to:

GiveWell is an independent, non-profit charity evaluator that performs in-depth research on charities to help people accomplish as much good as possible with their donations. You can donate to GiveWell's top rated charities through their website:

www.givewell.net

The International Planned Parenthood Federation is a global service provider and leading advocate of sexual and reproductive health and rights.

www.ippf.org

Opportunity International provides 'microloans' to entrepreneurs in some of the world's poorest nations. This not-for-profit organisation has a stunning 98 per cent repayment rate for its loans – which are then re-invested with other entrepreneurs and small business owners in developing nations.

www.opportunity.org

Oxfam International is a longstanding global organisation seeking to combat poverty and injustice around the world.

www.oxfam.org

Population Services International is a not-for-profit organisation that promotes products, services and healthy behaviour that enable low-income and vulnerable people to lead healthier lives, through initiatives such as distributing bed nets and condoms in developing countries where malaria and HIV/AIDS are major risks to life. (Note: at the time of writing GiveWell gave PSI its highest rating.)

www.psi.org

Note: I have no affiliations to any of the charities listed here. They are merely examples based on my past charitable donations.

Start giving *now*

I highly recommend checking out the calculator at http://www.thelifeyoucansave.com/calculator .

For many readers the amount suggested as a donation will only be **one per cent** of total income. I challenge anyone to present a valid reason why they *could not* donate this minimal amount.

Of course, if you can donate more, then please do.

Each month or pay period allocate a cause or charity to donate to and give the amount suggested, or more. It's that simple.

I love this simple act of giving (in addition to any philanthropic or charitable work I devote my time to) as something tangible that I can do to help my fellow man.

Give the gift of your time

Consider when you are able to give just a little of your time. Remember that charity is not always about giving money, and it's not even about donating your time to soup kitchens and volunteer programmes. The simple act of listening to someone who is lost and alone for a few minutes, instead of cutting them off and walking away, can be a valuable act of charity.

Charitable bill paying

When you receive a bill, rather than being angry, frustrated or otherwise negative about the process, begin to instead see it as an opportunity to be part of the great 'money-go-round' in which we all participate. Money and wealth are never really 'ours'; they are simply residing with us for a time as part of the inevitable in- and outflow of money. Money is energy, and it is a wonderful chance to give and receive love. Next time you have a bill, pay it with loving kindness, knowing it will help someone to pay their own bills, send their kids to school and put food on the table.

Visualisation

Lie or sit quietly and gently bring your attention to your breath. When you feel calm and centred imagine great quantities of wealth (in the form of money or however else you may imagine it) being attracted to you. As you feel the energy of this money coming to you, begin to release it and let it flow through you and back out into the universe. Release any and all attachments to holding on to the money, and instead come to peace that you are part of the flow, and you are a conduit for energy of all types – including money and wealth.

'… It is in giving that we receive.
It is in pardoning that we are pardoned.'
~ From the Prayer of St Francis of Assisi

Reflections

How much do I really give to my fellow man?

Do I give regularly? (In time and money)

Am I more concerned with accumulating than giving?

*Do I only give begrudgingly or out of obligation (a 'should')
or do I give freely and with joy?*

*Do I view taxes as a burden, or as a way of contributing
positively to my society?*

CHAPTER TWELVE

Conservation

The effect of global health on personal happiness

"WHEN WE HEAL THE EARTH, WE HEAL OURSELVES."

~ DAVID ORR

How does conservation make us happier?

We all know it's a 'good' thing to do, and we all know it's the 'right' thing to do, but what does that really mean?

It may even be that by now you are sick of all the talk about the environment, resources, climate change and emissions …

We all know that conserving the resources of our planet is going to be good in the long term, but for many people this simply isn't enough.

There is a set point of largesse in our prevailing paradigm of materialism and consumerism, a set point which is fundamentally at odds with conservation and waste reduction.

The prevailing paradigm supports the overuse of resources and the creation and hoarding of the inconsequential. This has only been 'sustainable' in the relative short term because relatively few people on the planet have lived at the level of usage and consumption that is the norm in the western world, whilst the great majority of people on the planet live in a much more abject state of poverty marked by subsistence.

In fact, the wealth and consumerism that marks the modern, developed world is only allowed in a sense by the fact that most people, on a global scale, are not actually able to live at this level. But as this changes, and as developing nations begin to reach higher levels of consumption in conjunction with population growth, resources will begin to dwindle more quickly, and pollution will rise exponentially.

This lack of sustainability will at some stage in the not-too-distant future begin to seriously hamper the quality of life for those of us in the western world who have become accustomed to living a life of relative luxury. And in saying this I am certainly not saying life is 'easy', but we certainly have, over the last 50 to 150 years transposed a prevailing paradigm of scarcity with one of abundance – but not always of the things that are truly important. This will change as resources become reduced and the relative demand for these scarce resources increases.

There is one simple way to reduce this effect – which in its logical extension will result in a large loss of quality of life, and therefore happiness, for us — and that is to conserve resources *now*, before it is too late.

Sustainability advocate Mathis Wackernagel has theorised that if everyone on the planet lived like North Americans, we would require five earths worth of resources to sustain our lifestyle[16].

Anyone can see that, as the world develops and developing nations also begin to take on the same consumer-driven lifestyle and infrastructural development, this situation will rapidly become *completely unsustainable*.

I must also make the case that this is completely *unfair*. That a large proportion of the world *must* live in abject poverty in order to allow us to live a life of wasteful largesse goes completely against my sense of natural justice. By continuing to turn a blind eye and allowing this to go on we are in fact propagating this disparity of health, happiness and wellness.

The reasons for not just needing to conserve, but more so *wanting to*, are huge, and would take a book in itself to investigate. Suffice to say, that given we are all interconnected and *all* responsible for the growth of the human spirit and the evolution of the human 'being', we cannot truly cultivate an environment of love and happiness in the absence of conservation.

---

[16] Note: Original blog post containing quote at http://earthsky.org no longer exists.

Biodiversity

Diversity of species and diversity *within* species is crucial to ensuring genetic stability and strength, and on a greater scale, preserving the ecosystems upon which we all rely for the planet to function properly. We now know quite unequivocally that the earth is like a huge organism with interdependent components that rely on the health of one another to survive. We would not expect to survive very long if we removed one of our essential organs, yet we expect the planet to survive the wholesale destruction of its parts, especially as there isn't time for it to adapt to these losses.

Climate change

Again, using the analogy of the body, we could not be expected to survive if our internal temperature were markedly raised or lowered. There is a fairly narrow range of homeostasis in which the body functions correctly, and therefore the planet, as it is now, also has this. Whether the planet could adapt quickly enough to relatively rapid changes in temperature in order to ensure the survival of its component parts is unknown, but it is far too costly a risk when our very survival is at stake.

Direct monetary effects on the individual

There are also tangible and direct monetary effects on our happiness from conserving our earth's valuable resources.

For many of us our transportation costs are one of our largest day-to-day expenses. Whether this is - the cost of fuelling and running our cars, or public transport, the cost stems primarily from the consumption of fossil fuels. Fuel is – until we find viable, renewable and sustainable options – a finite resource. As supply decreases and stocks dwindle, the laws of supply and demand dictate that resources will become more expensive, and therefore, as we have to spend more on transport, we will be less able to spend money on other things that provide us with experiences that enrich our lives. We may also have to work longer to make more money to cover these costs, thereby reducing the time available to do other things.

Increasing transport costs also reduce our ability to travel and experience new sights, sounds and tastes, all of which reduces our overall level of happiness and fulfilment.

Full disclosure: I admit that I have travelled a fair amount in my life and have therefore spent a lot of fuel on my personal adventures. This is a conundrum for many of the 'time rich' who are also eco-conscious. My justification to myself (accept it or not!) is that I am trying to reduce my use of resources wherever I can and also reduce unnecessary travel. As I become more involved in the eco-movement I am also, in spite of my passion for travel and adventure, beginning to travel long distances less, using planes less and finding other ways to experience adventures with less impact.

In our homes we can also reduce (completely inadvertently) the amount we have to spend on experiences by wasting water and electricity. The 'dripping tap' situation is no more apt than with an actual dripping or running tap.

Arguments Against 'Human-Driven Climate Change' v. Eco-Pragmatism

There is a very small but vocal minority amongst the scientific community and the public at large who doesn't believe that climate change is even occurring or that, if it is, it is merely a natural aberration and one not induced in any way by humans. I have in the past considered the evidence behind this viewpoint, and whilst not convinced myself, there is a bigger point that many people, both for and against, seem to have missed: **There is no good reason to pollute or waste resources.**

Even if you don't agree that global warming is being caused or exacerbated by carbon and other emissions, any realist and pragmatist would see it as absurd not to want to reduce emissions anyway.

These emissions cause the air pollution that kills more than 400 people every year in my home city of Auckland, New

Zealand[17] – which is considered to be extremely 'green' by world standards.

The World Health Organisation has stated that; "Air pollution is the environmental factor with the greatest impact on health in Europe and is responsible for the largest burden of environment related disease."[18]

It is clear that emissions and other waste affect our health. Global warming or not, that much is clear and there is no justification for wanton pollution.

It is also undeniable that we *will* run out of oil and other fossil fuels if our usage isn't *drastically* reduced. Again, there is controversy over how long it will take, but that is no good reason not to find an alternative. As always, groups with vested interests seem to be so preoccupied with stressing their opinion that we have *x* amount of years left of oil, they forget that those years are the only years available to find and instigate a viable alternative.

The common opinion that we *will* find an alternative is also flawed. I'm not saying that we won't find economically and technologically viable forms of alternative fuels, but we also cannot always take as a 'given' that we will always be able to come up with a timely technology-based solution whenever we are presented with a calamity. This faith in our human abilities

---

17

http://www.arc.govt.nz/albany/fms/main/Documents/Environment/Pollution/airfacts5.pdf

[18] European Environment Agency (2005), Environment and Health. EEA Report No. 10/2005

and ingenuity is laudable but is also potentially calamitous and begs the question, 'What if we don't find an answer to the problems *we* have created?'

The mentality of simply assuming that we will find answers to our current ecological problems assuages the fear of real and impending danger and permits wanton resource wastage to keep on occurring, all predicated on the assumption that, in Kiwi lingo, 'she'll be right mate!'

Energy usage in general, be it electricity, fossil or other fuels, has a direct effect on our environment – and as we have seen this has an effect on our individual states of health and happiness.

Those who know me know I am not an extremist. I am not your typical, sandal-wearing, bearded hippy (although I have occasionally worn sandals, I much prefer to walk barefoot, and beards get itchy). Extremism is just something I can't do. Whenever we develop ideas that are too extreme, we fall victim to becoming over dogmatic, and when we become dogmatic, we are, by nature, resistant to change, and hence we can't adapt. As change is constant, I have always felt a pragmatic approach to life works best, at least for me. I am a pragmatic environmentalist. The things I do to encourage my own health, that of my clients, and that of the planet, really have to be *affordable* and *realistic*.

There are many things we can do in our daily lives to 'leave only little footprints' – to lessen our effect on the world we live in. In a typical day we can make minor changes that

have a major net effect on our waste and resource usage.
Compare these two examples:

Usual Routine	Low Eco-Impact Routine
Rises and showers. Brushes teeth with water running.	Rises and showers. Brushes teeth – turns off water while brushing.
Quick breakfast of frosted cornflakes and milk.	Quick breakfast of organic muesli with organic free-range milk.
Goes to the gym – forgets to turn off lights in the house.	Walks to the gym or picks up a friend on the way – turns off lights first.
Gym session for 1½ hours. Recovery drink after training – tub is finished so throws in the trash.	Gym session for 1½ hours. Recovery drink after training – tub is empty so put it out for recycling.
Goes home to shower before work.	Showers at the gym before work.
Works all morning both on and off computer.	Works all morning both on and off computer – puts computer on 'power save' mode when not using.
Drives to café for lunch – buys a sandwich and coffee: total cost $8.	Walks to the park with home-made sandwich of whole grain organic bread, fresh organic salad greens and lean beef (NZ grass-fed!) and a coffee bought on the way: cost of meal approx.: $6.50 or less.
Continues working, has a 1-hr meeting with a client in the meeting room. Leaves computer	Continues working, has a meeting with a client in the meeting room. Turns off lights and 'hibernates' computer in the office.

and lights on.	Drives home at the end of the day.
Drives home at the end of the day.	Walks to local food store.
Drives to local food store.	Watches some television, turns it OFF at the set (not left on standby). Turns off cell phone. Reads for 30 mins and then goes to sleep.
Watches some television, goes to bed, reads for 30 mins and then goes to sleep.	

You can see that the 'standard' routine is not really that 'bad' and to all appearances does not seem wantonly wasteful, and conversely the more eco-friendly person is hardly the poster boy for the environmental movement – but there is still a large difference in the amount of waste and emissions created, and resources used.

In fact, by simply making a few minor changes, that have no impact on time, quality of life or enjoyment, the lower eco-impact routine has allowed this person to save at least:

Water ~ 1 litre

Petrol ~ 2.25 l ($4.43)

Power ~ 1710 W (360 + 1350 from 2 lights left on) (35c)

Food savings ~ $1.50

Total Savings in Dollars: $6.28

Approximate minimum savings per year: $1,507.20 (from working days alone)

There are many more things he could do but by taking just a few simple steps he has managed to be a lot eco-friendlier. He has eaten similar, if not identical foods, and performed the same work and the same recreational activities.

By making some minor changes in what we do day to day, and without becoming obsessed or obsessive, the results we achieve can be marked.

I can conceivably save well over $1,500 per year by simply walking more (50 mins walking time to my office and back) as compared to taking the bus or driving, along with savings from the simple actions listed above. If we factor in weekends at the same rate (many of us do a lot more travelling and eating in the weekends) I would save well over $2,500 per year, or enough to allow me to fly virtually anywhere on the globe.

Can't afford to travel?

But are you affording yourself the 'luxury' of waste?

I can save even more by making lunches (even if using supposedly expensive organic and free-range ingredients) rather than buying it.

Simply switching off appliances when not using them and not always relying on 'standby' mode saves loads of power, and by using the simple 'hibernate' or 'sleep' function on computers we can save even more energy and a lot of money along the way.

Of course, by doing even more, our impact on the world can be less and we can have substantially more money to spend on other things that improve the quality of our lives, and also more to give others to improve the quality of theirs.

There is no excuse for waste, particularly when the alternative costs us no more, either in terms of time or money.

'A living planet is a much more complex metaphor for deity than just a bigger father with a bigger fist. If an omniscient, all-powerful Dad ignores your prayers, it's taken personally. Hear only silence long enough, and you start wondering about his power. His fairness. His very existence. But if a world mother doesn't reply, Her excuse is simple. She never claimed conceited omnipotence. She has countless others clinging to her apron strings, including myriad species unable to speak for themselves. To Her elder offspring she says - go raid the fridge. Go play outside. Go get a job. Or, better yet, lend me a hand. I have no time for idle whining.'

~ David Brin

We are all connected, and our health, wellness and happiness are dependent on every other living and non-living thing on the planet. By conserving resources, we are allowing others the potential to have greater and cheaper access to resources essential for life. We are also minimising possible calamitous effects of resource scarcity on our children and our children's children. Like giving to charity, a culture of conservation we create in our own lives helps us to feel great.

Beginning to conserve can also be accomplished through simple, easy changes to daily activities that cost us no additional time or money.

Some simple, low cost/low time things you can do are:

Recycle

Nearly all our household waste can now be recycled. Almost all glass, most plastic, and paper and cardboard can all be recycled. Check your local council website to see which plastics can be recycled in your area, as the types of plastic that can be recycled are increasing.

Eat healthily!

Eating more natural, whole and unprocessed foods means your food will have taken up fewer resources (required to power processing plants). If you also choose more natural foods without packaging, such as fresh fruits and veggies, and use your own reusable bags – or simply ask for fewer bags at the checkout – your impact can be even greater.

Eat Organic

Organic foods are not necessarily healthful, and the processes of some organic manufacturers are every bit as damaging as 'traditional' ones, but they at least have the benefit of not using petrochemical fertilizers and pesticides. Where you are buying natural, whole and unprocessed foods that are *also organic* the net effect of your purchase is even better.

Eat 'sustainable'

Sustainable farms and growers try to run as close as possible to zero-input practices. They reuse and recycle material and waste. By doing this they are able, for example, to use compost waste and animal waste to fertilize fields, use excess grain and fodder as feed for livestock and use land cycling creatively to reduce or eliminate pesticide, fertilizer and herbicide use.

Eat local

It has been theorised that local fruits and veggies when in season have better levels of secondary nutrients. There is also less degradation in nutritional quality when the time to market is less. The planet also has less carbon emissions, resulting from the transport of food items over long distances, to cope with.

Switch off appliances

Unplug your cell phone charger.

Leaving appliances like these chargers plugged into the wall and switched on when they are not in use drains small amounts of electricity. Simply switch them off and/or unplug them, and you will waste less energy and save money in the long run.

Compost your food waste or get a worm farm

Food and other 'green' waste can account for nearly half an average family's landfill waste. A worm farm can take care of a lot of your food scraps and provide fertilizer for the garden, and a compost heap can take even more of your food waste and provides nourishing soil for the lawn or garden.

Grow your own lettuce and salad greens

Growing your own veggies saves money and ensures that your veggies are of the highest quality; however, not all of us have the time or inclination to have a full vegetable garden. But it is extremely easy to grow your own lettuce and salad veggies.

Why salad veggies? Because most of us eat so many of them anyway, and while they are healthful because of the micronutrients we get from them, they also have quite a big eco footprint; that is, we get very few calories from them, but many calories are expended (in the form of petrochemicals for fertilizers, pesticides and fuels) to first grow them and then get them to our table. Many of us also now buy 'bags' of lettuce or plastic salad boxes rather than heads of lettuce.

A landscape gardener acquaintance of mine says "There's no excuse *not* to grow your own lettuce!"

Anyone, no matter how small their apartment or condo, can grow lettuce and salad greens.

Simply get a large tray and fill with good quality soil or potting mix. Mix some mixed salad greens or lettuce seeds (about 4–6) with sand and sprinkle over the mix. Water, and in a few weeks, you will have some baby lettuces you can begin to eat. Alternatively, use a planter box (approx. 20–30 cm wide) and plant at a distance of one seed per 20-30 cm of length.

Wash your clothes using cold water

Clothing can be washed with cold water most of the time and only blasted by a hot wash very occasionally if necessary. Many fibre types and fabrics respond better to cold water anyway.

Use the dryer less

I noticed when I moved from the slightly more amiable climate in New Zealand to Vancouver, Canada, that my washing dried a lot less easily. I was forced to use the dryer more than I had in New Zealand (where I didn't even own one!). But even in the damper, darker climes of BC it is possible on many days – particularly during summer – to dry clothes on a line or clothes rack. The power savings are considerable.

The bottom line is that none of us are perfect and we are never going to be. The reality, though, is that many of us could save money and help the environment by doing a few simple things that take virtually no time yet still allow us to do everything we need to do.

Start looking around and seeing areas where you can reduce your impact on the planet – without driving yourself crazy!

Reflections

Do I think about the effects of my actions on the planet?

Are there simple, no-cost ways I could reduce my use of resources and reduce my waste output?

Do I buy new things when something I have would do the job just as well?

Do I recycle?

Live the Shit Out of Life

"DON'T BROOD! GET ON WITH LIVING AND
LOVING. YOU DON'T HAVE FOREVER ..."
~ LEO BUSCAGLIA

One cannot be happy if one is constantly worrying about the future or feeling guilt and remorse about the past. Just as surely no one can be happy who predicates his or her sense of satisfaction and self-worth on what others say and on past glories. To be free and to have the life of our dreams – a life of happiness, a life defined by joyous, wonderful experiences, we actually have to be there. We have to be complete and present in the moment, and we have to be having moments doing the things we love, and *really*, really doing them.

I have become known for the quote that lends itself to the title of this chapter ...

You really just have to **live the shit out of life** if you're really going to live at all. In fact there really is no other way!

One day I was talking with my sister over a breakfast catch-up, as she was in a bit of a funk and needed a little advice from her little brother. We had a great discussion and as she was about to leave and head off to work I said, "You know what, Char – can you do just one thing for me?"

To which she replied, "OK … what's that?"

"Just LIVE THE SHIT OUT OF TODAY!"

This spin on my favourite affirmation whilst not being awfully 'PC' does perfectly and vociferously encapsulate the concept of *really* living life and living it to the full, with passion and purpose.

You just can't be half-hearted about life if you are really living the shit out of it!

I am reminded of the audio book *Wild at Heart* by Tessa Bielecki – the wonderful Carmelite nun who, when speaking about mindfulness and being complete in the moment, recalls Zorba the Greek asking himself 'What am I doing now?' with the idea that whatever he is doing, he should *really* do it.

I often ask the same question.

And the answer can always be: *I am doing the shit out of something!* – whatever that something is.

A short time ago I was walking to work and I found myself worrying about something quite inconsequential and something I had no control over at that moment.

So I stopped myself and asked, "What am I doing now?"

The reply of course was, "I am WALKING the SHIT out of this path!" And just after slipping back into a more mindful, purposeful state I looked down and narrowly avoided stepping in a big pile of dog crap. So by walking the shit out of that path I literally avoided stepping in shit.

My question to you is: Are you living the shit out of life? …

Why not?

Because let's face it – it's easy to be alive. Alive is the default. You didn't need to do much to wake up this morning.

But to live, to really *live* – well, that takes the courage to choose to do it, to accept that you may have to step outside the norm and live by your own set of rules.

So … just f***in' do it.

'You have your brush, you have your colors, you paint paradise, then in you go.'

~ Nikos Kazantzakis

EPILOGUE

In writing this book I wanted to highlight what I feel to be a flawed paradigm that we have fallen into.

Time is our most important currency; money, on the other hand, merely provides the means by which we procure our immediate survival needs and provides additional comfort to us and those around us. It further acts as a conduit by which we enable experiences. It is *those* experiences that provide the golden moments of joy that make a life worth living.

We need to satisfice, and we need to realise when 'good enough' is 'good enough'. We also, I believe, need to find joy in daily life. We need to cultivate the mindfulness and awareness that allows us to appreciate the beauty around us and connect with the wonderful souls we encounter each and every day.

People are seldom satisfied with where they are in life, and this is often seen in a negative light. The idea of complete satisfaction seems to be the goal for many. But it is a goal that is never set and worked towards, and even if it were it would ultimately be unattainable.

Dissatisfaction can be the foundation, providing the initial impetus for each of us to reach towards our goals, our dreams and take advantage of our ambitions. The key, though, is to approach our dissatisfaction with mindfulness and realise that although we may not be entirely *satisfied* with where we currently stand in any area of our life, we can be *happy* right now, right here and with the things we currently have.

In other words, we can be happy even if we are not completely satisfied.

Satisfaction really is by nature a transient concept. After a great meal, for example, we say to ourselves, "Wow, I really am satisfied," but a few hours later we are again hungry. Perhaps a better word is 'content'. I am content with where I am, but at times I may not be wholly satisfied with my lot in life, so I have the power to choose to change it, all the while enjoying the journey as it unfolds. It's a matter of perception but I think we overcomplicate what is important in life. To my mind the point of life is to be happy.

Yes, it's that simple. Many people I say this to laugh and think that it's over simplistic. *But what is more important in life than creating joy and love?*

Feeling fulfilled, happy, purposeful. These are all faces of the very same dice. So how are you going to roll it?
Some people are fortunate enough to be born into wealth. Others are fortunate enough not to have to deal with illness or death of loved ones. But people who don't have at least some

degree of hardship, trial or tribulation in this life are rare indeed. In many ways it is the trials and hardships of life that make us more 'human'. They allow us to take that important step of putting ourselves in other people's shoes, thereby creating empathy. It is this empathy that can provide the mental, emotional and spiritual shift that moves us away from a life of being status and possession driven towards one of experience.

When we reach our final moments on this earth what do you think we will remember and enjoy the memory of? Will it be the long hours at work and toiling to finish that report? Will it be remembering those lazy afternoons wasted watching infomercials because you really didn't know what to do?

And when we shuffle off this mortal coil what do you think you will want to surround you: your medals, your degrees and diplomas, your brand-new Porsche? Or your family and friends, the people you have loved, and who have loved you?

And so, it begs the question – if you want to be surrounded by the people you love at your time of death, to remember the wonderful experiences you gave yourself over a life lived to the full – why not start it now? If not now, when?

There are things I have never regretted in life. Spending time with loved ones and travel are the things that immediately spring to mind. And although I try to live a life without regrets – a life that is lived on purpose, there are times when I know I have made poor choices. Those poor choices are almost always the ones that disconnected me from the people around me and the world I live in, and the times when I have forsaken experiences that could have enriched my life.

We are all born 'time equal'.

You have 24 hours in your time account.
How are you going to spend it?

Be prepared but expect nothing. Accept unfolding events with palms and lips upturned.
Blessings & aroha nui e hoa ma
~ Cliff

<h1 style="text-align:center">BIBLIOGRAPHY</h1>

Allen, David. 2002, *Getting Things Done,* Penguin, New York.

Aristotle, Revised Edition, 2009, *The Nicomachean Ethics, Oxford World Classics,* Oxford University Press, New York.

Beers, Emily. "Cliffdog has landed" <u>The Performance Advocate</u> Nov. 2007. Email e-zine to database. 27 Nov. 2007

Beilecki, Tessa. *Wild at Heart.* Audio book read by author. Louisville, CO: Sounds True, 2006

Bond, Michael. *The Pursuit of Happiness.* <u>New Scientist.</u> 4 Oct. 2003. <http://www.newscientist.com/article/mg18024155.100-the-pursuit-of-happiness.html>

Cameron, Julia. 1992, *The Artists Way,* Tarcher, New York

Das, Surya, 2000, *Awakening to the Sacred,* Three Rivers Press, New York.

Doidge, Norman. 2007 *The Brain that Changes Itself,* Penguin, New York.

"Environment and Health." <u>European Environment Agency</u> EEA Report No. 10: (2005)

Ernsberger, Richard. *Behind the Smile; Can poor people be more self-satisfied than the rich? New clues to an old mystery.* <u>Newsweek International</u> 26 July 2004. <http://www.highbeam.com/doc/1G1-119580297.html>

Ferriss, Timothy. 2007, *The 4 Hour Workweek,* Crown Archetype, New York.

"Fortune 500" <u>CNN Money.com</u> 3 May. 2010. <http://money.cnn.com/magazines/fortune/fortune500/2010/full_list/101_200.html>

Gilbert, RM. "Caffeine Consumption." <u>Progress in Clinical Biological Research</u> 158 (1984): 185-213

Godin, Seth. *Linchpin.* Audio book read by author. New York: Random House Audio, 2010

Goebel, M U et al. "Behavioural conditioning of antihistamine effects in patients with allergic rhinitis." <u>Psychotherapy and Psychosomatics</u> 77.4 (2008): 227-34

Harvey, Cliff. 2009, *Choosing You! How you can choose to live the life of your dreams ... RIGHT NOW!,* CC Publishing, Auckland.

Harvey, Cliff. *Stop Getting Through*. <u>Cliffdog.com</u> 23
Feb. 2010.
<http://cliffdog.blogspot.com/2010/02/stop-getting-
through.html>

Harvey, Cliff. *Training Movements Not Muscles.*
<u>Cliffdog.com</u> 14 Nov. 2009.
<http://cliffdog.blogspot.com/2009/11/training-
movements-not-muscles.html>

Hawkins, David, 1995, *Power vs Force,* Veritas
Publishing, West Sedona, AZ.

"Health Effects of Air Pollution" <u>Auckland Regional
Council</u> June. 2007.
<http://www.arc.govt.nz/albany/fms/main/Document
s/Environment/Pollution/airfacts5.pdf>

Kearns, D W. Crossma, J. "Effects of cognitive
intervention package on the free-throw performance of
varsity basketball players during practice and
competition." <u>Perceptual Motor Skills </u>75.3 pt 2 (1992):
1243-53

Kelly, Kevin. *1,000 True Fans.* <u>The Technium </u>March
2008.
<http://www.kk.org/thetechnium/archives/2008/03/1
000_true_fans.php>

Lipton, Bruce, 2008, *The Biology of Belief,* Hay House, New York.

Marquez, Gabriel Garcia. 2003 *Living to Tell the Tale,* Knopf, New York.

New Testament. Psalms. Proverbs. New American Standard Bible North Guelph, ON: Gideons International, n.d.

"Panera: Pay what you can afford." St Louis Business Journal 19 May. 2010. <http://www.bizjournals.com/stlouis/stories/2010/05/17/daily21.html>

Pert, Candace, 1999, *Molecules of Emotion,* Simon & Schuster, Chicago.

Pinchot, Gifford. *The Gift Economy.* Pinchot & Company n.d. <http://company.pinchot.com/MainPages/BooksArticles/OtherArticles/GiftEconomy.html>

Ranganathan, V K et al. "From mental power to muscle power – gaining strength by using the mind." Neuropsychologia 42.7 (2004): 944-56

Schmidt-Traub, S. Baumler, K J. "The psychoimmunological association of panic disorder and allergic reaction." <u>British Journal of Clinical Psychology</u> Feb:36.1 (1997): 51-62

Sogyal Rinpoche, 1994, *The Tibetan Book of Living and Dying,* Harper One, New York.

"Success" <u>Oxford Dictionry Online</u> <Oxford Dictionary Online:
http://www.oxforddictionaries.com/definition/success?view=uk>

Thich Nhat Hanh, 1994, *The Miracle of Mindfulness,* Beacon Press, Boston.

United States Bureau of Labour Statistics. <u>American Time Use Survey.</u> (news release) 24 June 2009. <http://www.bls.gov/news.release/archives/atus_0624 2009.htm>

Wikipedia. <u>The Gold Standard.</u> <http://en.wikipedia.org/wiki/Gold_standard#Post-war_international_gold-dollar_standard_.281946.E2.80.931971.29>

World-English.Org <u>The 500 Most Commonly Used Words in the English Language.</u> <http://www.world-english.org/english500.htm>

Useful Websites & Online Reading

By the Author

www.cliffharvey.com

www.cliffdog.com

www.barefootandbedless.com

Happiness and Inspiration

www.brite-talk.com

www.everydayspirits.com

www.awakeningsource.blogspot.com

Simplicity and Minimalist Abundance

www.lessdoing.com

www.zenhabits.net

www.4hourworkweek.com

Multi-Locational & Non-Locational Living

www.globallifestyleproject.com

Conservation Resources

www.myfootprint.org

Charity

www.thelifeyoucansave.com

www.givewell.org

ABOUT THE AUTHOR

When **CLIFF HARVEY** isn't wandering barefoot, having epiphanies whilst surfing or regaling beautiful women with

fanciful tales over a glass of fine wine, he is a naturopath, author and speaker.

In over 13 years in practice he has helped thousands around the globe to live happier, healthier lives and continues to inspire through his writing, speaking and personal spiritual and life purpose mentoring.

When not lecturing, writing or in private clinical practice you might find Cliff competing at a world championship level in All-Round weightlifting, training with professional MMA fighters, bouncing at bars, or road managing rock bands.

It's all experience … and that's the stuff life's made of! And if all else fails you'll find him blissfully dozing on Takapuna Beach, Auckland, New Zealand or Kitsilano, Vancouver, BC. For more information about Cliff Harvey, go to www.cliffharvey.com

www.ingramcontent.com/pod-product-compliance
Lightning Source LLC
Chambersburg PA
CBHW021245060726
47590CB00005B/1910